DEVELOPMENT

access to geography

DEVELOPMENT

Garrett Nagle

Hodder Murray

A MEMBER OF THE HODDER HEADLINE GROUP

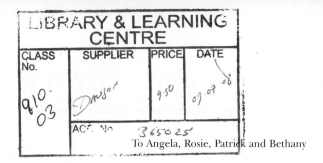
To Angela, Rosie, Patrick and Bethany

The publishers would like to thank the following for permission to reproduce copyright material: Routledge, for extracts from *The Environment: Principles and Applications* by C Park (1997) used on pages 115 and 117.

All photos by the author.

Every effort has been made to trace all copyright holders, but if any have been inadvertently overlooked the Publishers will be pleased to make the necessary arrangements at the first opportunity.

Although every effort has been made to ensure that website addresses are correct at time of going to press, Hodder Murray cannot be held responsible for the content of any website mentioned in this book. It is sometimes possible to find a relocated web page by typing in the address of the home page for a website in the URL window of your browser.

Orders: please contact Bookpoint Ltd, 130 Milton Park, Abingdon, Oxon OX14 4SB. Telephone: (44) 01235 827720. Fax: (44) 01235 400454. Lines are open 9.00 - 5.00, Monday to Saturday, with a 24-hour message answering service. Visit our website at www.hoddereducation.co.uk

Copyright © Garrett Nagle 2005
Third edition published in 2005 by
Hodder Murray, an imprint of Hodder Education,
a member of the Hodder Headline Group,
an Hachette Livre UK Company,
338 Euston Road, London NW1 3BH

First Published 2005
Impression number 10 9 8 7 6 5 4 3
Year   2010 2009 2008 2007

Cover photo shows water development in Antigua, photo by Garrett Nagle
Typeset in Baskerville 10/11pt and produced by Gray Publishing, Tunbridge Wells
Printed in Malta

A catalogue record for this title is available from the British Library

ISBN 978 0 340 88487 4

Contents

1 Development and Underdevelopment

1 Defining Development

The term 'development' is difficult to pin down. It refers to an improvement in a number of characteristics, but not necessarily in all of them. It suggests advances in:

- demographic (population) conditions, such as falling birth rates and increasing life expectancies

Figure 1 Tokyo fish market – the consumption of fish resources here is not sustainable

- economic progress such as increased **gross domestic product (GDP)**, **gross national income (GNI)** or **purchasing power parity (PPP)**
- social improvement such as greater equality for women, better race relations, and greater participation in the political process.

Development also suggests improved personal freedom and quality of life, and, implicitly, greater access to, and use of, natural resources (Figure 1). Increasingly, definitions of development entails some notion of environmental management – to what extent the environment is used in a **sustainable** fashion (Figure 2).

Goulet (1971) has distinguished three basic components that must be included in any true meaning of development: life sustenance, self-esteem and freedom:

- **Life sustenance** is concerned with the provision of basic needs such as housing, clothing, food and minimal education.
- **Self-esteem** is concerned with the feeling of self-respect and independence. A country cannot be regarded as fully developed if it is exploited by others, or cannot conduct economic relations on equal terms. Colonialism has now virtually ended, but some would argue that there are modern equivalents of colonialism, i.e. neocolonialism. For example, the International Monetary Fund (IMF) and World Bank dominate economic policy making in many LEDCs. Also, transnational corporations (TNCs) that operate in many LEDCs

Figure 2 Sustainable development in Barbados – recycling of
old tyres for a herb garden

often introduce consumption patterns and techniques of production that do not have the interests of the LEDC at heart.

- **Freedom** refers to the ability of people to determine their own des-
tiny. No person is free if they are imprisoned on the margin of subsistence without education and skills.

The term **poverty** is closely linked to development. Deprivation with
respect to income, health, education, social life and/or environmental quality can be called poverty.

Poverty can be divided into **absolute and relative poverty**. Absolute
poverty is measured against a benchmark – such as the cost of getting
enough food to eat. Relative poverty is measured against society's
standards; in LEDCs the basket of 'essentials' comprises food and a
few items of clothing, whereas in MEDCs it includes holidays, presents
and entertainment.

2 Classification of Global Economic Groupings

An early, and not very useful, classification of development was to
divide the world into three main groups:

- The First World: developed – western Europe, North America,
Australia, New Zealand and Japan.
- The Second World: state-controlled Communist countries such as
the former Soviet Union.
- The Third World: developing – all the other less-developed countries.

A more popular and detailed way is as shown in Figure 3.

More economically developed countries (MEDCs): such as the UK and
the USA are the most 'developed' countries and have high standards of
living.

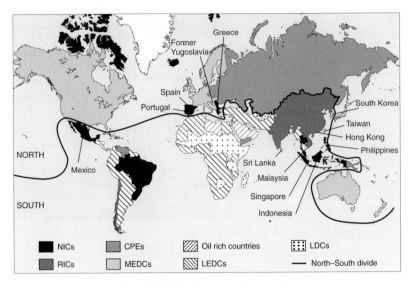

Figure 3 Global economic groupings

Centrally planned economies (CPEs) are socialist countries such as North Korea strictly controlled by the government. Living standards are higher than many LEDCs, although freedom of speech is limited. Many former Communist countries (FCC) remain in this category.

Oil-rich countries include Saudi Arabia and Libya. These countries are very rich in terms of GNP per head, although it may not be distributed very evenly. Without oil many of these countries would be LEDCs.

Transition economies include newly industrialising countries and recently industrialising countries. **Newly industrialising countries (NICs)** include the original Asian 'Tiger economies', e.g. South Korea and Taiwan. These are countries that have experienced rapid industrial, social and economic growth since 1960. (By contrast **old industrial countries (OICs)** are usually MEDCs.) **Recently industrialising countries (RICs)** are those that have followed the same path as NICs only more recently, such as Chile.

Less economically developed countries (LEDCs) are at a lower stage of development and have a lower quality of life, e.g. Namibia and Egypt. These can be subdivided into middle income and low income LEDCs. **Least developed countries (LDCs)** include Afghanistan and much of sub-Saharan Africa, where standards of living are very low, as are most indicators of development. LDCs realised average improvements in life expectancy, child mortality and literacy rates until the 1980s, more recent statistics have shown, however, that these improvements were less valid for the poorest of these countries and, more specifically, for the lowest income groups. In fact, in the 1980s there was a reversal in some of the development indicators.

	MEDC	NIC	Oil rich	RIC	LEDC	LDC	CPE	Third World Socialist
Example	UK	South Korea	Saudi Arabia	India	Egypt	Mozambique	North Korea	Zimbabwe
GNP/capita ($)	24,390	8690	6500	450	1430	230	1000	1900
Economic growth (%)	2.5	5.7	1.6	6.0	4.4	6.2	1.00	−13.6
Population growth (%)	0.21	0.85	3.7	1.51	1.66	1.13	0.98	0.68
Infant mortality rate (‰)	5.45	7.58	49.5	61.5	58.6	138		29.84	67.08
Computers/100 people	33.8	19.0	5.7	0.5	1.2	–	–	1.7
Doctors/1000 people	1.7	1.3	1.7	0.4	1.6	0.025	–	0.14
Population below poverty line (%)	17	4	N/A	25	23	70	–	70

Figure 4 Development table for selected countries

Since the early 1990s a sub-set has been officially recognised as the '**heavily indebted poor countries**'.

Other important groupings include OPEC, G7, G8 and G10 countries. **OPEC** (the Organization of Petroleum Exporting Countries) represents the interests of oil exporters. Its position is undermined by some oil-producing countries such as the UK, who do not agree with OPEC-controlled oil prices. The **G7/8** is a group of the world's wealthiest and most powerful countries. The G7 includes Japan, the USA, France, Italy, the UK, Germany and Italy. G8 countries are those of the G7 and Russia. The **G10** or **Paris Club** is a collection of 11 countries. These are the wealthiest members of the International Monetary Fund (IMF), and include Belgium, Canada, France, Germany, Italy, Japan, the Netherlands, Sweden, Switzerland, the UK and the USA.

More developed countries, such as the UK, the USA and Japan, have high levels of the indicators shown in Figure 4. By contrast, countries that are less developed have lower levels. The **north–south divide** describes the difference in wealth between the developed world and the developing world. The **development gap** is the increasing inequality in levels of development between the north and the south.

3 Changing Ideas About Development

(a) Modernisation

In the 1950s, as Europe reconstructed after its war-time losses, most other countries developed as a result of state-directed **modernisation**.

'Development' implied that less economically developed countries (LEDCs) modernised and gradually assumed the qualities of the more economically developed countries (MEDCs).

(b) Dependency Theory

From the late 1960s modernisation theory was challenged by the Latin American **dependency school** and the **world systems school** that highlighted the weak structural position of Third World countries in the world system (see pages 30–32). For example, multinational or transnational companies (TNCs) became increasingly powerful and used their economic and political power to exploit or suppress less powerful, more vulnerable nations. Dependency ideas rejected Western modernisation/development as corrupting and destructive or as a continuation of colonial forms of domination.

In the 1980s and 1990s, the introduction of cultural studies to the study of development was a significant change as it abandoned a Eurocentric development thinking (i.e. development as catching up and imitation) and, instead, considered development as an inclusive, liberating process, in which different forms of development are accommodated.

Thus, despite 50 years or so of development initiatives, results have been very disappointing: there remains massive underdevelopment, exploitation and repression, the debt crisis, famine, increasing poverty, malnutrition, violence and global terrorism.

(c) Post-modernism

According to the **post-modernist** approach, the role of the state is being weakened from above as well as from below. There is increasing importance of international political organisations that interfere politically, and also militarily in particular states. There is also the growing importance of the global financial market. Economically, the state is seen as disappearing as an economic actor through privatisation and deregulation.

The **basic needs approach** searched for more human-centred and locally relevant processes and patterns of development. In short, under the basic needs approach, development was redefined as a broad-based, people-oriented or endogenous process, as a critique of modernisation and as a break with past development theory.

(d) Participatory Development

Participatory development means that local people participate in every stage of the development process – planning, implementation and evaluation. According to the strongest advocates of participatory development, 'normal' development is characterised by biases – Eurocentrism, positivism (prediction) and top-downism – that are disempowering. The flipside is that 'non-expert', local people were sidelined and their only role was as the objects of grandiose schemes.

Nevertheless, there are problems with participatory development:

- tokenism: as participatory development has become popular, some agencies use the rhetoric of participation with limited empowerment
- much participatory development has treated communities as socially homogenous
- the emphasis on civil society can create competition between local organisations
- participatory development seeks to give local people control, but many processes affecting their lives are often not readily tackled at the local level.

4 Measuring Development

The most commonly reported development statistic is a country's GDP (gross domestic product), GNP (gross national product) or GNI (gross national income) per capita.

Approximately 15% of the world's population live in areas with a high GNP/capita. The map of GNP/capita shows a clear bias towards MEDCs. Western Europe, North America, Japan and Australia come out on top: the highest values are:

- Luxembourg $55,100
- the USA $37,800
- Norway $37,700.

Fifty-six per cent of the world's population live in areas classified as having a low GNP/capita. Moreover, a number of countries have a GNP/capita of less than $500 per year. These are the LDCs and include East Timor, Sierra Leone and the Gaza Strip. Reasons for their stagnation include:

- civil wars and territorial disputes
- rapid population growth
- paying off previous debt
- a lack of resources
- natural and human hazards (including AIDS).

However, political mismanagement or war is a major cause of their economic stagnation.

This picture of a largely rich north and a largely poor south is an oversimplification. For example, within the north there is a significant east–west divide. Parts of the former Soviet Union (FSU) and eastern Europe (the 'Second World') have experienced a great deal of economic chaos since the fall of the Berlin Wall in 1989. The formerly highly protected economies have been opened up to a degree of free-market enterprise, but in many cases the economies have crumbled. Lack of hard currency and a devalued currency have caused widespread shortages of money in the FSU.

Within the south there is also considerable variation. As well as the LEDCs there are some countries that are relatively well off. NICs such as South Korea and Taiwan have quite high levels of GNP/capita. The development of the original Asian tigers is the result of a combination of state-led industrialisation, spontaneous industrialisation and TNC-led industrialisation.

There are a number of problems in using these indices:

- as an average, the statistic takes no account of distribution
- GDP is an income measure that ignores other dimensions of development
- they do not show regional variations
- they do not show ethnic and racial variations in GDP/capita
- they do not take into account the local cost of living, unlike purchasing power parity (PPP)
- they fail to pick up the social and environmental costs of development.

CASE STUDY: WORLD POVERTY

In terms of absolute poverty, the World Bank and other sources have reported an overall decline, based on the $1-a-day standard, to almost half of the reported figure in 1981 (33% in 1981 to 18% in 2001) (see Figure 5). This decline is not occurring throughout all LEDCs however, and there are reports that the number of people living in poverty is increasing in Africa from one in 10 in the 1980s to one in three today. There are also questions over whether the actual numbers of those considered to be in absolute poverty have declined.

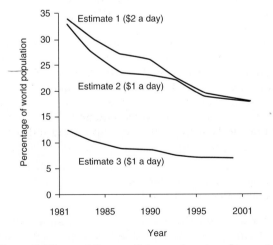

Figure 5 The world's poor living on less than $1 per day: (above) expressed as a percentage of the world's population and (opposite page) as a number shown by region

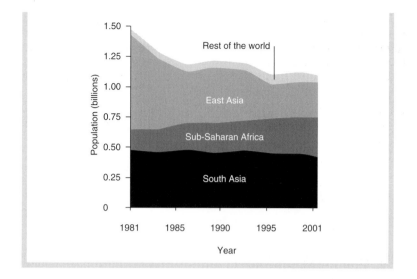

(a) Alternative Measures of Development

The thinking of Goulet and Sen (1983) has led to the construction of alternative measures of economic and social development to supplement statistics on growth rates and levels of per capita income of countries. Over the years a number of composite measures of development have been suggested. The physical quality of life index (PQLI), has been superseded in recent years by the United Nations Development Programme's (UNDP's) human development index (HDI) and the human poverty index (HPI), published in its annual *Human Development Report.*

The **human development index** (HDI) is a simple summary measure of three dimensions of development: living a long and healthy life, being educated and having a decent standard of living. It therefore combines measures of life expectancy, literacy and income to allow a broader view of a country's development than using income alone (i.e. GDP or GNI), which is too often equated with well-being. Since the creation of the HDI in 1990 three supporting indices have been developed to highlight particular aspects of human development:

- **human poverty index** (HPI)
- **gender-related development index** (GILL)
- **gender empowerment measure** (GEM).

The HDI can highlight the successes of some countries. For example, Venezuela started with a higher HDI than Brazil in 1975 (0.72 vs 0.64), but Brazil has made much faster progress (both now 0.755). Finland had a lower HDI than Switzerland in 1975 (0.84 vs 0.87) but has moved marginally ahead (0.930 vs 0.925).

High levels of human development can be achieved without high incomes and high incomes do not guarantee high levels of human development. Pakistan and Vietnam have similar incomes (about $2000), but Vietnam has a much higher HDI (0.69 vs 0.5). Similarly, Jamaica has a similar income to Morocco (about $3600–3700), but a much better HDI (0.76 vs 0.6).

Swaziland has approximately the same HDI as Botswana (0.55 vs 0.61) with less than two-thirds of the income ($4200 vs $7900), and the same is true of the Philippines and Thailand. Thus, with the right policies, countries can advance human development even with low incomes.

(b) Trends in HDI

Most regions have seen steady improvement in HDI over the past decade, with east Asia and the Pacific performing particularly well. Arab states have also seen substantial growth, exceeding the average increase for LEDC. Sub-Saharan Africa, by contrast, has been almost stagnant. Two groups of countries have suffered setbacks:

- FSU countries going through a long, painful transition to market economies
- poor African countries whose development has been hindered or reversed for a variety of reasons – including HIV/AIDS and internal and external conflicts.

Comparing the ranking of developing counties by their HDI and gross national income show some interesting patterns. Many oil-producing countries, for example, have much lower HDI rankings than their GNI rank, while some poor countries rank relatively high by their HDI because they have deliberately devoted scarce resources to human development. Countries such as Cuba (0.806), Costa Rica (0.832), Vietnam (0.688) and Sri Lanka (0.730) fall into this category.

(c) Human Poverty Index

The UNDP's **human poverty index** (Figure 6) is also based on three main indices: the percentage of the population not expected to survive beyond the age of 40 years, the adult illiteracy rate and a deprivation index based on an average of three variables – the percentage of the population without access to safe drinking water, the percentage of the population without access to health services and the percentage of children under the age of 5 years who are underweight through malnourishment. Many of the world's poorest people live in such bad conditions that it is difficult for those fortunate to live in MEDCs to comprehend what it means to be poor. The UNDP has calculated that the cost of eradicating poverty across the world is relatively small compared to global income – not more than 0.3% of world GDP – and that political commitment, not financial resources, is the real obstacle to poverty eradication.

Index	Longevity	Knowledge	Decent standard of living	Participation or exclusion
HDI	Life expectancy at birth	(1) Adult literacy rate; and (2) combined enrolment ratio	GDP per capita (PPP US$)	–
HPI-1	Probability at birth of not surviving to age 40 years	Adult illiteracy rate	Deprivation in economic provisioning, measured by: (1) percentage of people without sustainable access to an improved water source; and (2) percentage of children under 5 underweight for age	–
HPI-2	Probability at birth of not surviving to age 60 years	Percentage of adults lacking functional literacy skills	Percentage of people living below the income poverty line (50% of median adjusted disposable household income)	Long-term unemployment rate
GDI	Female and male life expectancy at birth	(1) Female and male adult literacy rates; and (2) female and male combined primary secondary and tertiary enrolment ratios	Estimated female and male earned income, reflecting women's and men's command over resources	–

Figure 6 HDI, HPI-1, HPI-2 and GDI: same components, different measurements

While the HDI measures overall progress in a country in achieving human development, the human poverty index (HPI) reflects the distribution of progress and measures the backlog of deprivations that still exist. The HPI measures deprivation in the same dimensions of basic human development as the HDI. It is divided into two indices as described below.

HPI-1
The HPI-1 measures poverty in LEDCs. It focuses on deprivations in three dimensions:

- longevity, as measured by the probability at birth of not surviving to 40 years of age
- knowledge, as measured by the adult illiteracy rate

- overall economic provisioning, public and private, as measured by the percentage of people not using improved water sources and the percentage without sustainable access to an improved water source and the percentage of children underweight for their age.

HPI-2

Since human deprivation varies with the social and economic conditions of a community, a separate index, the HPI-2, has been devised to measure human poverty in selected OECD (Organization for Economic Co-operation and Development) countries, drawing on the greater availability of data. The HPI-2 focuses on deprivation in the same three dimensions as the HPI-1 and one additional one, social exclusion. The indicators are:

- probability at birth of not surviving to 60 years of age
- adult functional illiteracy rate
- percentage of people living below the income poverty
- long-term unemployment rate (12 months or more).

(d) Gender-related Development Index

The gender-related development index (GILL) measures achievements in the same dimensions and using the same indicators as the HDI, but examines inequalities between women and men. It is simply the HDI adjusted for gender inequality.

(e) Gender Empowerment Measure

The gender empowerment measure (GEM) reveals whether women can take active part in economic and political life. It exposes inequality in opportunities in selected areas. It focuses on participation, measuring gender inequality in key areas of economic and political participation and decision making. It tracks the percentages of women in parliament, among legislators, senior officials and managers, and among professional and technical workers, and the gender disparity in earned income, reflecting economic independence. Norway is ranked first in the GEM (0.837) and Yemen seventieth (0.127). The UK is seventeenth with 0.675; Bangladesh is sixty-ninth with 0.218.

5 Income Poverty

Extreme poverty declined only slowly in developing countries during the 1990s: the share of the population living on less than $1 a day fell from 28% in 1987 to 23% in 1998, and the number of poor people remained roughly constant as the population increased. The share and number of people living on less than $2 per day – a more relevant threshold for middle income economies such as those of east Asia and Latin America – showed roughly similar trends.

Regions	Population covered by at least one survey (%)	Number of people living on less than $1 a day (millions)			
		1987	1990	1998 new	1998 (GEP 2000)
East Asia and the Pacific	90.8	417.5	452.4	267.1	278.3
(excluding China)	71.1	114.1	92.0	53.7	65.1
Eastern Europe and central Asia	81.7	1.1	7.1	17.6	24.0
Latin America and the Caribbean	88.0	63.7	73.8	60.7	78.2
Middle East and north Africa	52.5	9.3	5.7	6.0	5.5
South Asia	97.9	474.4	495.1	521.8	522.0
Sub-Saharan Africa	72.9	217.2	242.3	301.6	290.9
Total	**88.1**	**1183.2**	**1276.4**	**1174.9**	**1198.9**
(excluding China)	84.2	879.8	915.9	961.4	985.7

	Population covered by at least one survey (%)	Headcount index (%)			
		1987	1990	1998 new	1998 (GEP)
East Asia and the Pacific (excluding	90.8	26.6	27.6	14.7	15.3
China)	71.1	23.9	18.5	9.4	11.3
Eastern Europe and central Asia	81.7	0.2	1.6	3.7	5.1
Latin America and the Caribbean	88.0	15.3	16.8	12.1	15.6
Middle East and north Africa	52.5	4.3	2.4	2.1	1.9
South Asia	97.9	44.9	44.0	40.0	40.0
Sub-Saharan Africa	72.9	46.6	47.7	48.1	46.3
Total	**88.1**	**28.3**	**29.0**	**23.4**	**24.0**
(excluding China)	84.2	28.5	28.1	25.6	26.2

Figure 7 Population living on less than $1 per day and headcount index in developing countries, 1987, 1990 and 1998.
Source: www.worldbank.org/poverty accessed 16 July 2004

In general, poverty declined in countries that achieved rapid growth, and increased in countries that experienced stagnation or contraction. Indeed, the overall decline in extreme poverty during the 1990s was driven by high rates of growth in countries with large numbers of poor people. For example, China accounted for a quarter of the total number of poor at the start of the decade, and per capita

GDP during the 1990s rose by 9% per year, so by 1998 China's share of the world's poor was less than a fifth. Nevertheless, the decline in poverty in rapidly growing countries was slowed by increases in inequality in a number of countries with large numbers of poor, in particular in China, India, Bangladesh and Nigeria.

6 The Development Gap

Since 1970 there has been a dramatic improvements in LEDCs. Overall, life expectancy increased by 8 years, illiteracy has been cut nearly in half, to 25%, and in east Asia the number of people surviving on less than $1 a day was almost halved.

However, for many countries the 1990s were a decade of despair. Over 50 countries are poorer now than in 1990 (e.g. Democratic Republic of Congo), and in 21 countries a larger proportion of people is malnourished, e.g. Democratic Republic of Congo and Burundi. In 14 countries, child mortality rates have increased, e.g. Zimbabwe and Botswana, while in 12 countries primary school enrolments have shrunk, e.g. Democratic Republic of Congo and Iran. In 34, life expectancy has fallen, largely due to AIDS, e.g. Botswana. A further sign of a development crisis is the decline in 21 countries in the human development index (HDI), a summary measure of three dimensions of human development – living a long and healthy life, being educated and having a decent standard of living. In addition, the long-term development gap has increased (Figure 8). Banking has influenced this latest list, with Luxembourg, Bermuda and the Cayman Islands benefiting from a very strong banking sector.

Richest					
1820		*1900*		*2003*	
UK	$1756	UK	$4593	Luxembourg	$55,100
Netherlands	$1561	New Zealand	$4320	USA	$37,800
Australia	$1528	Australia	$4299	Norway	$37,700
Austria	$1295	USA	$4096	Bermuda	$36,600
Belgium	$1291	Belgium	$3652	Cayman Islands	$35,000
Poorest					
1820		*1900*		*2003*	
Indonesia	$614	Myanmar	$647	Malawi	$600
India	$531	India	$625	Palestine	$600
Bangladesh	$531	Bangladesh	$581	Sierra Leone	$500
Pakistan	$531	Egypt	$509	Somalia	$500
China	$523	Ghana	$462	East Timor	$500

Figure 8 World's richest and poorest countries, 1820–2003
(GDP per capita, US$)

South and east Asia contain the largest numbers of people in poverty, although both regions have made gains. In the 1990s China lifted 150 million people – 12% of the population – out of poverty, halving its incidence. By contrast, in Latin America and the Caribbean, the Arab states, central and eastern Europe, and sub-Saharan Africa the number of people surviving on less than $1 a day increased.

(a) UN Goals

UN goals are often dismissed as overly ambitious and rarely achieved. Yet many goals have been achieved (Figure 9).

(b) Regional Contrasts in Development

Stark differences are emerging between regions, with some regions pulling ahead and reaching new levels of development, while others are falling behind. The same pattern is occurring within regions: some countries are succeeding amid disappointing regional trends, while others are falling behind in regions making good overall progress.

South Asia remains one of the world's poorest regions. Because it is so heavily populated, it is home to the largest number of poor people. More than 33% of south Asians lack access to improved sanitation, 33% live in poverty, 25% go hungry, 20% of children are out of primary school and almost 10% of children die before 5 years of age.

Nevertheless, significant progress was made in all these areas in the 1990s, lifting the region from the basement of development. Except for Afghanistan, no country experienced reversals in the key indicators for the Millennium Development Goals. However, there was some divergence: Bangladesh and Bhutan reduced their under-5 mortality rates by more than 6%, and Nepal by more than 5%. India's performance varied enormously across states, with inequality increasing between several states, such as Maharashtra at the top end, and Rajasthan, Uttar Pradesh, Madhya Pradesh and Bihar at the other.

Like south Asia, sub-Saharan Africa faces enormous poverty. Unlike south Asia, it is falling behind. Almost all African economies have faltered: half of Africans live in extreme poverty and one-third in hunger, and about one-sixth of children die before 5 years of age. With low completion rates, only one in three children in the region finish primary school. Yet amid this picture of stagnation and reversals, some countries achieved impressive progress in the 1990s. In Mauritius, Mozambique and Uganda per capita income grew by more than 3% a year, and Ghana and Mozambique achieved some of the world's sharpest reduction in hunger. In the face of HIV/AIDS, 10 countries reduced child mortality by 3% or more – Malawi by more than 5%.

In contrast, Latin America and the Caribbean have HDI levels approaching levels in MEDCs. Nevertheless, despite progress in some areas (education, under-5 mortality), the 1990s saw slow economic growth and slight increases in poverty. There was great variation in

Successes

- Eradicating smallpox (World Health Organization declaration, 1965) – achieved in 1977
- Immunising 80% of infants (before their first birthday) against major childhood diseases by 1990 – achieved in about 70 countries, although the achievements have not been maintained in sub-Saharan Africa and south Asia
- Reducing children's deaths from diarrhoea by half – achieved in the 1990s
- Cutting infant mortality to less than 120 per 1000 live births by 2000 – achieved in all but 12 developing countries
- Eliminating polio by 2000 – more than 175 countries are now free of this disease
- Eliminating guinea-worm disease by 2000 – by 2000 the number of reported cases had declined by 97%, and the disease has been eliminated in all but 14 countries

Significant progress has been made on many other goals even though they were not fully achieved

- Accelerating economic growth in developing countries to 5% per year by the end of the 1960s and to 6% in the 1970s – during the 1960s, 32 countries exceeded 5%, and during the 1970s, 25 countries exceeded 6%
- Increasing developing countries' share in global industrial production – the share rose from 7% in 1970 to 20% in 2000, although these gains were limited to a small number of countries.
- Raising life expectancy to 60 years by 2000 – achieved in 124 of the 173 countries that fell below this threshold (almost all of them among the least developed countries, with many in sub-Saharan Africa).
- Reducing child mortality by at least one-third more during the 1990s – 63 countries achieved the goal, and in more than 100 countries child deaths were cut by 20%
- Eliminating or reducing hunger and malnutrition by 2000 – in developing countries malnutrition dropped 17% between 1980 and 2000, but in sub-Saharan Africa the number of undernourished people rose by 27 million in the 1990s
- Achieving universal access to safe water by 1990, then by 2000 – access increased by 4.1 billion people, reaching 5 billion

Failed goals

- Increasing official development assistance to 0.7% of rich countries' GNP starting in 1970 – assistance has actually fallen as a share of GNP, and in the 1990s only four countries achieved the 0.7% target (Denmark, the Netherlands, Norway and Sweden)
- Allocating 0.15% of GNP for official development assistance to the least developed countries in the 1980s and 1990s – eight of 16 members of the OECD's Development Assistance Committee achieved the 0.15% target in the 1980s, but only five of 20 did so in the 1990s
- Halving adult illiteracy by 2000 – illiteracy fell from 25% in 1990 to 21% in 2000
- Eradicating malaria – although there was success in Asia and Latin America, the 'global' anti-malaria programme of the 1960s largely bypassed Africa (due to the perceived intractability of the disease there) even though it suffers the largest malaria burden. Over the next several decades the international community devoted little attention and scant resources to malaria, leading to fragmented interventions

Figure 9 UN goals – successes and failures

the proportions of malnourished populations: the proportion of hungry people almost tripled in Cuba, from 5% to 13%, while Peru had the region's biggest reduction, from 40% to 11%. Under-5 mortality rates fell in Bolivia (from 12% to 8%) and Ecuador (from 6% to 3%), while Barbados and Jamaica experienced almost no improvement.

(c) Trends in Global Inequality

The Human Development Report 2002 noted that while the definition of global income inequality is vague and its trends ambiguous, there is widespread consensus on its grotesque levels. The 25 million richest people living in the USA have as much income as almost two billion of the world's poorest people.

International inequality is generally measured by comparing national per capita incomes. Countries with the highest per capita incomes in the early 1800s are still today's richest countries. In 1820 western Europe's per capita income was 2.9 times Africa's – and in 1992, 13.2 times. In the 1990s per capita incomes increased slowly but steadily in high-income OECD countries. At the same time, highly populated developing countries such as China and India achieved rapid growth. However, many transition economies in central and eastern Europe, particularly the Commonwealth of Independent States (CIS), many parts of sub-Saharan Africa and some countries in Latin America and the Caribbean experienced economic stagnation.

Income surveys suggest that global inequality has increased since the 1980s. The main forces behind this divergence were:

- a widening income gap between the poorest and the richest people due to slow growth in rural incomes in populous Asian countries relative to rich OECD countries
- faster progress in urban China relative to rural China and to India
- shrinkage in the world's middle-income group.

But these conclusions are not entirely conclusive due to the limited timeframe covered. Using alternative methodologies, other analysts have reached more optimistic conclusions suggesting convergence in global individual incomes: that after peaking in 1970, the gap in 1995 had returned to the level in 1950.

(d) Inequality Across People Within Countries

In many countries inequality in income appears to be on the rise. Between the 1980s and the mid- to late-1990s inequality increased in 42 of 73 countries with complete and comparable data. Only six of the 33 developing countries (excluding transition economies) in the sample saw inequality decline, while 17 saw it increase. In other words, within national boundaries control over assets and resources is increasingly concentrated in the hands of a few people.

Although not the case for all these countries, in many inequality began increasing during the debt crisis of the early 1980s. Since then inequality has soared, particularly in the CIS and south-eastern Europe. And in many Latin American countries inequality remains extremely high.

CASE STUDY: INEQUALITY IN THE UK

Findings based on the 2001 census found that over the past decade many skilled workers had migrated from the north to find work in London, mainly in the booming financial services industry and this, along with the growth of the capital, was attributing to an increasing north–south divide.

Not all are in agreement with these findings, however, and state that there has been a recent regeneration of northern cities like Liverpool and Manchester. However, smaller towns are indeed suffering from industrial decline and figures suggest that there was a 5% increase in the number living in poverty in these areas in 2001 from a decade earlier.

CASE STUDY: INEQUALITY IN CHINA

In recent decades China has shown large disparities in economic and social outcomes between coastal and inland regions – a pattern that also reflects differences between urban and rural areas. Coastal areas have consistently experienced rapid economic growth. Between 1978 and 1998 per capita incomes increased by 11% per year, and increased in the 1990s, with annual growth averaging 13% – five times the level in China's slowest-growing north-western regions. As a result the bulk of national income is concentrated in metropolitan and coastal regions (Figure 10).

In 1999 China's three richest metropolises, Shanghai, Beijing and Tianjin, were near at the top of the HDI ranking. Those at the bottom were all western provinces. Moreover, the poorest provinces have the highest inequality – Tibet had the lowest values for education attainment and life expectancy.

After an improvement in rural incomes in China in the 1980s due to the decentralising of power and planning and the encouragement of rural enterprise, the inequality between rural and urban areas is growing again, with incomes in urban areas averaging three times more than those in rural areas. Coupled with this, the increase in unemployment in rural areas due to the closure of businesses suffering from the competition in urban

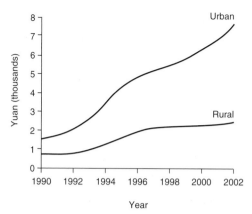

Figure 10 China: more national income is concentrated in metropolitan and coastal regions. *Source*: National Bureau of Statistics of China

areas and bad investment is exacerbating the economic difference between the two areas. The difference in earning power is threatening to destabilise the social system as rural dwellers, now able to move to the cities after the restrictions on mobility were removed, are unable to afford basic needs such as housing in the urban areas.

7 Development Challenges

Figure 11 describes the world divided into five categories:

- countries with high economic innovation, as measured by the number of patents per million people – these tend to be the high-income countries
- LEDC exporters of manufactured goods – in 1995 at least half of these countries' exports were in the manufacturing sector
- fuel-exporting economies
- transition countries
- commodity (non-fuel)-exporting developing countries.

Figure 12 breaks down patterns of economic growth by economic structure. Grouping countries in the same five categories as Figure 11, it shows that the main problems in economic growth have come in three types of economies: transition countries, oil-exporting economies (which faced a huge loss of purchasing power from their single or dominant export commodity) and commodity (non-fuel)-exporting developing countries. Most of the commodity-exporting countries are in sub-Saharan Africa, Latin America and central Asia. Innovating

Group	Countries that grew in GDP per capita	Average annual growth in GDP per capita (%)
Technology innovators	18 out of 18	1.7
Transition countries	4 out of 12	−1.7
Fuel exporters	2 out of 13	−1.5
Manufacturing exporters	23 out of 24	2.7
Commodity (non-fuel) exporters	29 out of 61	−0.1

Figure 11 Economic growth rates by country group, 1980–1998

Geographic location	Small countries			Large countries		
	Countries that grew in GDP per capita	Average annual growth in GDP per capita (%)	Population living in countries that grew, 2001 (millions)	Countries that grew in GDP per capita	Average annual growth in GDP per capita (%)	Population living in countries that grew, 2001 (millions)
Inland populations	24 of 53	−0.2	379 of 799	10 of 10	2.5	3087 of 3087
Coastal populations	15 of 17	1.9	118 of 130	3 of 4	3.2	341 of 418

Figure 12 Economic growth rates by population size and location, 1980–1998. *Note*: GDP per capita is measured in purchasing power parity. Small countries are those with fewer than 40 million people. Coastal countries are those in which at least 75% of the population are within 1000 km of the coast

economies and manufacturing exporters among developing countries by and large experienced economic growth.

Figure 11 highlights patterns of economic growth geographically. Groups of countries that are large or coastal experienced higher average per capita economic growth from 1980 to 1998. Small and inland countries enjoyed much less economic success. In Africa, 33 of the 53 countries are small and inland.

(a) Geographic Distribution of Absolute Poverty

The majority of the world's poor people live in Asia. That majority is reduced, however, if attention is focused on the poorest quarter rather than the poorest one-third, for vast numbers in China and India and many in south-east Asia lie between these two. Conversely, the great majority of the countries in which more than half the population live in poverty are in Africa, whatever criteria are used to determine this.

The trend over recent decades clearly differentiates much of south and east Asia from most of tropical Africa. While no clear trend to either intensification or alleviation of poverty can be determined for most parts of tropical Africa over the past 30 years, there is very clear evidence of alleviation in many parts of east and south Asia. In India, for example, not only have average incomes risen, but also the proportion of households below any given income level has fallen. There has been similar improvement in almost all aspects of social welfare.

This poverty alleviation in Asia has, of course, occurred in a context of rising total population numbers; and so the absolute numbers of poor people, and hence the absolute amount of poverty, have remained fairly constant. However, the rate of population increase has been even greater throughout tropical Africa, so that there the absolute amount of poverty has increased massively, and continues to increase, whatever methods of measurement are adopted.

Chapter Summary

- The term 'development' is difficult to define and encompasses many values.
- Sustainable development is long-term development that improves basic living standards without compromising the needs of future generations.
- Increasingly, definitions of development see development as more than just economic growth.
- There are many classifications of countries – the most simple are the north–south divide and First-, Second- and Third-World countries. More detailed classifications include CPEs, NICs, LEDCs, LDCs, etc.
- Ideas about the appropriateness of development models have changed since the 1950s Eurocentric modernisation theories.
- Development is now seen as being inclusive and improving human welfare and conditions.
- Development is measured in many ways – GDP, GNP, GNI, PPP, HDI – each of which has its own strength and weakness.
- Global poverty – however measured – is widespread, and the development gap is increasing.
- There are many contrasts in development – some between countries and some within countries.
- Countries showing most growth in recent years are large countries and coastal countries.

Questions

1. Suggest and justify a definition of the term *development*.
2. Explain how and why ideas about *development* have evolved over time.
3. Suggest and justify a classification of countries, by levels of development, using the data in Figure 4.
4. Study the photograph below. Make a list of questions about the photograph. What does the image suggest about development? Give reasons to support your answer.

2 Strategies of Development

1 Causes of Underdevelopment

There are many causes of underdevelopment. These include war, natural hazards, unfair trading arrangements, corruption, lack of resources, colonialism, malnutrition, and poverty and inequality.

(a) War

War affects development in many ways. Not only are people killed and injured – especially young males of working age – funds are directed into the war effort that would otherwise have supported other projects. Crops are not harvested, infrastructure is destroyed, and supplies of food and water become unreliable. Many of the world's poorest countries have experienced war in recent years, e.g. Mozambique, Angola, Democratic Republic of Congo, Rwanda, Afghanistan and Palestine.

(b) Natural Hazards

Natural hazards may thwart a country's attempt to develop. The continuing volcanic eruption on Montserrat (see Chapter 6), the devastation of Hurricane Jeanne in Haiti, the effects of the south Asian tsunami in 2004, the long-term droughts of the Sahel in Africa prevent countries from fulfilling their potential. Land cannot be farmed, topsoil is eroded or destroyed, and the country becomes a net importer of food. As young, innovative people leave the area, there is a decline in the quality and quantity of labour. The reoccurring floods in Bangladesh are considered later.

(c) Trade

Many LEDCs are caught in unfair trading arrangements that keep them poor. As many LEDCs tend to export low-value primary products, and import expensive manufactured goods and services, they are worse off than their MEDC counterparts. In addition, many **trading blocs**, such as the European Union (EU) or the North American Free Trade Agreement (NAFTA), make it difficult for LEDCs to trade openly and competitively, so they remain impoverished.

(d) Corruption

The misuse of power can cause a country to remain impoverished. Despite earning millions in oil revenue, the bulk of Nigeria's population remained trapped in poverty, as it is alleged that much of the wealth has been embezzled by senior finance ministers. The seizure of Asian-owned businesses by Idi Amin in Uganda in 1973 or the seizure of white-owned farms and farms of people unsupportive of the Zimbabwe government are good examples. The diversion of funds in Iraq into the private accounts of Saddam Hussein resulted in low investment in other parts of the economy.

(e) Lack of Resources

Some countries, such as Namibia and Eritrea have failed to develop due to a lack of significant resources. Others, such as Botswana, have done well from minerals such as diamonds. Singapore is an excellent example of a country that has developed despite a lack of resources. The country managed to use its favourable geographical location to act as a transport hub for much of the Pacific rim.

(f) Colonialism

According to some commentators, many African countries have passed from being fairly well off to being less developed. This is due to colonialism, in which the imposition of taxes (and the seizure of lands) forced indigenous people to work for very low wages in the white-owned economy. A good example was the imposition of hut taxes in the eastern Cape of South Africa that forced indigenous Xhosa to work for whites, and lose their independence and wealth.

(g) Malnutrition

Malnourishment over sustained periods of time leads to problems with growth and development of the body, including the brain. This stunting of mental and physical capacity leads to problems within the workforce, as workers are weak, and as a result less productive. Thus, malnutrition can be seen as a cause, as well as a result, of poverty.

(h) Poverty and Inequality

Not all LEDCs are incapable of developing their economy autonomously, i.e. without help from the wealthier nations. India and China have both shaken off the socialist ideals that held them back and embraced capitalist ideology (although China remains politically communist) and experienced economic growth over the last decades both with regard to their domestic economy and international trade.

As the case study below shows, the causes of underdevelopment in any one area are unique and varied.

CASE STUDY: SUDAN AND BANGLADESH

Sudan and Bangladesh are both countries suffering from under-development, but it is for very different reasons. Sudan has been in the midst of a civil war for the past 20 years, which has caused widespread devastation to much of the country, including farm-land, and has led to widespread famine and malnutrition of the population. It is estimated that 1000 people are dying every day as a result of hunger-related diseases.

Bangladesh has been the victim of several severe floods that have destroyed crops and affected millions. The 2004 floods saw 31 million people affected and 600 lose their lives.

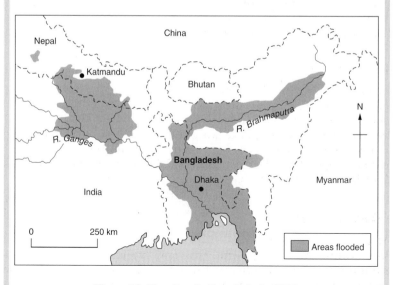

Figure 13 Flooding in Bangladesh, 2004

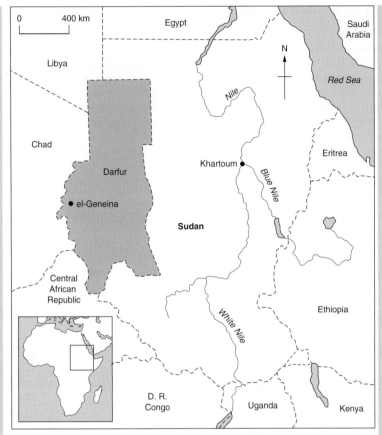

Figure 14 Darfur, Sudan. In this region 1.2 million people have been made homeless and 1000 are dying each day as a result of the civil war

2 Explaining Inequalities in Development

Models are ways of breaking down the complexities of real-life situations, and explaining how something works in simple terms. Many models focus on just one factor, and so are very simplified versions of reality. They do, however, allow us to look at a complex process and to understand at least part of it.

(a) Rostow's Model of Development (1960)

W.W. Rostow, a US economist, envisaged five stages in the development of an economy (Figure 15). His model is a useful starting point in describing and understanding levels of development. Five levels can be described. In the first, the traditional subsistence economy,

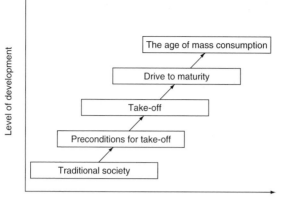

Figure 15 Rostow's stages of economic growth

there is an agricultural basis, little manufacturing and few external links. There are low levels of population growth (stage 1 of the demographic transition model (DTM)).

During stage 2, preconditions for take-off, external links are developed and resources are increasingly exploited, often by colonial countries or by multinational companies (MNCs). The country begins to develop an urban system (often with primate cities) and a transport infrastructure. Meanwhile, inequalities develop between the growing core and the underdeveloped periphery. Overall the population continues to increase (stage 2 of the DTM).

In stage 3, the take-off to maturity (or sustained growth), the economy expands rapidly, especially exported manufactured goods. Regional inequalities intensify because of multiplier effects. Economic growth can be 'natural' (as in the case of most MEDCs), 'forced' (the ex-socialist countries of eastern Europe) or planned (as in the NICs).

The drive to maturity, stage 4, sees the diversification of the economy, the development of the service industry (health, education, welfare, etc.), and growth spreads to other sectors and to other regions in the country. Population growth begins to slow down and stabilise (late stage 3 or early stage 4 of the DTM). Ireland, Greece, Spain and Portugal are at this level. Finally, in stage 5, the age of high-mass consumption, there are advanced urban-industrial systems, and high production and consumption of consumer goods, such as televisions, compact disc players, dishwashers, etc. Population growth slows considerably (stage 4 of the DTM). The UK and Germany characterise this level.

The main weaknesses of Rostow's model are:

- it is **anglo-centric**, based on the experience of North America and western Europe

- it is **aspatial** and does not look at variations within countries as a whole. For example, within the UK there are great disparities in the levels of development between the north and the south – Rostow's model fails to pick this out.

(b) Clark's Sector Model

According to Clark's **sector model** (1940) all MEDCs have progressed from agricultural societies to industrial and service economies. For some, such as the UK, the transition was early, mostly in the nineteenth century. By contrast in others, such as Ireland, it occurred during the twentieth century. The model clearly shows the transition from an economy dominated by the **primary sector** to one dominated, in turn, by the **secondary** and **tertiary** sector (Figure 16). Change occurs because success in one sector produces surplus revenue, which in turn is invested into new industries and technologies. These increased the range of industries in an area. For example, the cotton industry in the UK encouraged textile machinery, other metallurgical industries and service industries. The sector model is descriptive and offers only a crude level of analysis. It does not say how or why the country developed, nor does it show internal variations within the country.

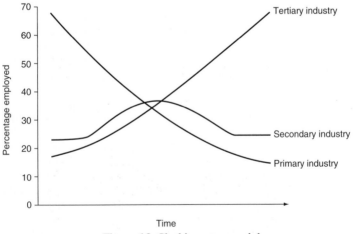

Figure 16 Clark's sector model

(c) Growth Poles

A growth pole is a dynamic and highly integrated set of industries organised around a leading industry or industrial sector. It is capable of rapid growth and generating **multiplier effects** or spillover effects into the local economy. The idea was originated by Perroux (1971). It has been widely used in regional and national planning as a means of regenerating an area. They can, however, increase regional inequalities by concentrating resources in favoured locations.

In these policies, places or districts that are favoured due to location, resources, labour or market access are more attractive and consequently developed by planners. They form natural **growth poles** and expand faster than other districts. Generally these are urban-industrial complexes that have good transport and accessibility. Dunkerque and Marseilles-Fos in France and Taranto in the Mezzogiorno, southern Italy are good examples of growth poles.

(d) Friedmann's Stages of Growth

Friedmann's stages of growth model was developed in 1966 (see Figure 17). In stage 1, the preindustrial economy, there are independent local centres and no hierarchy. This is similar to Rostow's stage 1. In stage 2, the transitional economy, a single strong centre

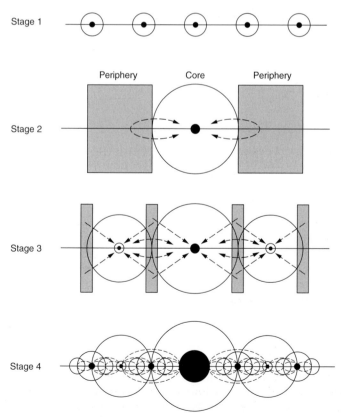

Figure 17 Friedmann's core–periphery model

emerges. This dominates the colonial society as the stage of preconditions begins. A growing manufacturing sector encourages concentration of investment in only a few centres – hence a core emerges with a primate city. Over time, an industrial economy (stage 3) develops with a single national centre, strong peripheral sub-centres, increased regional inequalities between core and periphery, and an upward spiral in the core and a downward spiral in the periphery. In time, as the economy expands, more balanced national development occurs – sub-centres develop forming a more integrated national urban hierarchy.

Finally, in stage 4, the post-industrial economy, there is a functionally interdependent urban system and the periphery is eliminated. Friedmann believed that stage 4 has been reached in the USA, although there are still peripheral areas such as the Ozarks, Appalachians and Alaska.

3 Alternative Models of Development

Many of the above theories were considered to be too focused on development patterns among MEDCs. A group of theories emerged that looked at development patterns in LEDCs and how the path differed from those in MEDCs. Nevertheless, these theories stressed how development issues in LEDCs were closely linked to what was happening in MEDCs.

(a) Dependency Theory

According to the **dependency theory**, countries become more dependent on more powerful, frequently colonial, powers, as a result of interaction and 'development'. As the more powerful country exploits the resources of its weaker colony, the colony becomes dependent on the stronger power. Goods flow from the colony to support consumers in the overseas country.

Andre Frank (1966) described the effect of capitalist development on many countries as 'the development of underdevelopment'. The problem of poor countries is not that they lack the resources, technical know-how, modern institutions or cultural developments that lead to development, but that they are being exploited by capitalist countries.

The dependency theory is a very different approach to most models of development:

- it incorporates politics and economics in its explanation
- it takes into account the historical processes of how underdevelopment came about, that is how capitalist development began in one part of the world and then expanded into other areas (imperialistic expansion)

- it sees development as a revolutionary break, a clash of interests between ruling classes (bourgeoisie) and the working classes (proletariat)
- it stresses that to be developed is to be self-reliant and to control national resources
- it believes that modernisation does not necessarily mean Westernisation, and that underdeveloped countries must set goals of their own, appropriate to their own resources, needs and values.

(b) World Systems Analysis

World systems analysis is identified with Immanuel Wallerstein (1974) and is a way of looking at economic, social and political development. It treats the whole world as a single unit. Any analysis of development must be seen as part of the overall capitalist world economy, not on a country-by-country approach. Wallerstein argued that an approach that looked at individual countries in isolation was too simplistic and suffered from **developmentalism**. The developmentalism school assumed that:

- each country was economically and politically free (autonomous)
- all countries follow the same route to development.

As such they were **ethnocentric**, believing that what happened in North America and Europe was best and would automatically happen elsewhere.

According to Wallerstein, the capitalist world system has three main characteristics:

- a global market
- many countries, which allow political and economic competition
- three tiers of countries.

The tiers are defined as **core**, largely MEDCs, the **periphery**, which can be identified with LEDCs, and the **semi-periphery** (Figure 18). The semi-periphery is a political label. It refers to those countries where there are class struggles and social change, such as Latin America in the 1980s and eastern Europe in the late 1980s and early 1990s.

Wallerstein argued that capitalist development led to cycles of growth and stagnation. One of these cycles is a long-term economic cycle known as a Kondratieff cycle. This identifies cycles of depression at roughly 50–60-year intervals. The last two were in the 1920s–1930s and the late 1980s. Stagnation is important for the restructuring of the world system and allows the semi-periphery to become involved in the development process.

Capitalism, according to the world system's approach, includes feudalism and socialism. They are extreme variations on the division of labour. As the world develops and changes, there will either be swing towards a more socialist system, or there will be a transition towards a more unequal (feudal) system.

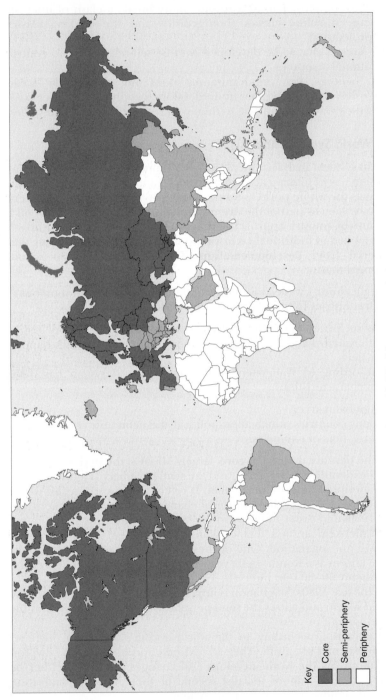

Figure 18 World systems analysis

Key

■ Core

▨ Semi-periphery

□ Periphery

4 Strategies for Change

There are a number of types of development that can help countries to develop. Two of the most well known are top-down and bottom-up development.

However, when these ideas are applied to the world's poorest continent, Africa, the prospects for development do not always seem quite so straightforward.

Top-down development	Bottom-up development
Usually large scale	Small scale
Carried out by governments, international organisations and 'experts'	Labour-intensive
Done by people from outside the area	Involves local communities and local areas
Imposed on the area or people by outside organisations	It is run by the locals for the locals
Often well funded and can respond quickly to disasters	There is limited funding available
Local people are not involved in the decision-making process	Local people are involved in the decision-making process
Emergency relief can be considered top-down	Common projects include building earthen dams, creating cottage industries

Figure 19 Top-down and bottom-up development

CASE STUDY: DEVELOPING AFRICA'S ECONOMY

The biggest challenges to many African countries are still poverty, hunger, disease and high birth rates, which leave the countries vulnerable to humanitarian disasters. Even the more politically stable countries, like Uganda, which have the leadership in power to be able to move the country forward economically, are held back by the poor infrastructure. The lack of roads, teachers, health care and electricity mean that countries are still unable to provide basic needs, e.g. enough food to feed the population. Until such needs are addressed, foreign investment is a distant hope.

Investment in preventative rather curative medicines would dramatically improve the plight for many African countries. Estimates on providing the funds for infrastructure, health care and improving education for selected African countries are far less than the average for non-African LEDCs (see Figure 20).

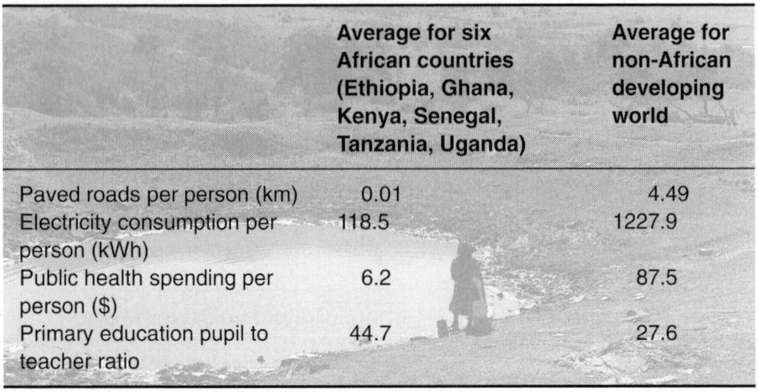

	Average for six African countries (Ethiopia, Ghana, Kenya, Senegal, Tanzania, Uganda)	Average for non-African developing world
Paved roads per person (km)	0.01	4.49
Electricity consumption per person (kWh)	118.5	1227.9
Public health spending per person ($)	6.2	87.5
Primary education pupil to teacher ratio	44.7	27.6

Figure 20 Infrastructure in Africa and other developing regions

Chapter Summary

- There are a number of causes of underdevelopment – war, famine, lack of resources and natural hazards for example.
- Each underdeveloped country has a unique set of factors causing it to be underdeveloped, e.g. Sudan and Bangladesh.
- There have been a number of models attempting to explain underdevelopment. These include traditional modernisation models, as well as alternative models such as Frank's and Wallerstein's.
- There are a number of strategies for development – some are 'top-down' and others are 'bottom-up' – and developing Africa's economy illustrates a number of such options.

Questions

1. For a country or region you have studied outline the reasons for its lack of development.
2. Critically assess the relevance of modernisation models (e.g. Rostow) to our understanding of the causes of development.
3. Outline the role of natural hazards in the process of underdevelopment.

3 Population and Food Supply

1 Population

(a) Fertility

The **crude birth rate (CBR)** is defined as the number of live births per 1000 people in a population. The CBR is easy to calculate and the data are readily available. However, it does not take into account the age and sex structure of the population. By contrast, the **standardised birth rate** gives a birth rate for a region on the basis that its age composition was the same as the whole country.

The **total fertility rate** is the average number of births per 1000 women of child-bearing age. It is the completed family size if fertility rates remain constant. The **general fertility rate** is the number of births per 1000 women aged 15–49 years. The **age-specific birth rate (ASBR)** is the number of births per 1000 women of any specified year groups.

In general, highest fertility rates are found among the poorest countries, and very few LEDCs have made the transition from high birth rates to low birth rates. Most MEDCs, by contrast, have brought the birth rate down. In MEDCs fertility rates have fallen as well – the decline in population growth is not therefore due to changing population structure.

(b) Changes in Fertility

Changes in fertility are a combination of both **socio-cultural** and **economic** factors. While there may be strong correlations between these sets of factors and changes in fertility, it is impossible to prove the linkages or to prove that one set of factors is more important than the other.

CASE STUDY: FERTILITY IN THE ARAB WORLD

Arab countries have seen a dramatic fall in the number of births per woman, for example the average number in Oman has fallen from 10 to less than four. This trend has been attributed to a number of factors, which include a greater emphasis on women having careers and thus delaying marriage until their 30s. The number of women married before the age of 20 has halved over the last 30 years.

(c) Level of Education and Material Ambition

In general, the higher the level of parental education, the fewer the children. Poor people with limited resources or ambition often have large families. Affluent families can afford large families – in general the middle-income families with the high aspirations but limited means tend to have the smallest families. They wish to improve their standard of living, and will limit their family size to achieve this (see Figure 21).

(d) Political Factors and Family Planning

Most governments in LEDCs have introduced some programmes aimed at reducing birth rates. Their effectiveness is dependent on:

Education level	Fertility rate per 1000	Average no. of births
University	42.18	1.15
Senior middle school	63.88	1.23
Junior middle school	67.43	1.44
Primary school	86.25	2.02
Illiterate	94.50	2.44

Figure 21 Women's educational level and births:
evidence from China

- focusing on family planning in general and not just specifically on birth control
- investing sufficient finance in the schemes
- working in consultation with the local population.

Where birth controls have been imposed by the government, they are not successful (except in the case of China). In the MEDCs, financial and social support for children is often available to encourage a **pronatalist** approach. However, in countries where there are fears of negative population growth (as in Singapore), more active and direct measures are taken by the government to increase birth rates.

(e) Economic Prosperity

The correlation between economic prosperity and the birth rate is not total, but there are links. As GDI increases, the total fertility rate generally decreases (Figure 22), and as GNP/head increases so the birth rate decreases (Figure 23). Economic prosperity favours an increase in the birth rate, while increasing costs lead to a decline in the birth rate. Recession and unemployment are also linked with a decline in the birth rate. This is related to the cost of bringing up children. Surveys have shown that the cost of bringing up a child in the UK can be over £200,000, partly through lost earnings on the mother's part. Whether the cost is real, or imagined (perceived), does not matter. If parents believe they cannot afford to bring up children, or that by having more children it will reduce their standard of living, they are less likely to have children.

At the global scale, a strong link exists between fertility and the level of economic development, with the UN and many NGOs believing that a reduction in the high birth rates in the LEDCs can only be achieved by improving the standard of living in those countries.

(f) The Need for Children

High infant mortality rates increase the pressure on women to have more children. Such births are termed replacement births or compensatory

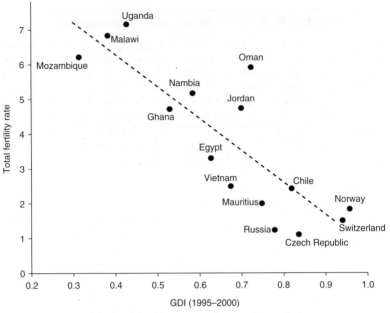

Figure 22 Total fertility rate and gross domestic income

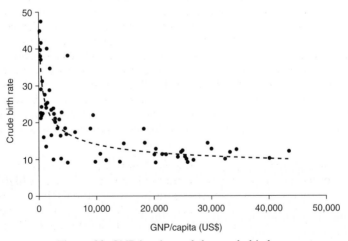

Figure 23 GNP/capita and the crude birth rate

births to offset the high mortality losses. In some agricultural societies, parents have larger families to provide labour for the farm and as security for their old age. This is much less important now as fewer families are engaged in farming, or as many farmers are labourers rather than owning their own farms.

2 Population Mortality

The **crude death rate** (CDR) is the number of deaths per 1000 people in a population. The CDR is a poor indicator of mortality trends: populations with a large number of aged people, as in most MEDCs, will have a higher CDR than countries with more youthful populations. Examples are Denmark 11‰ and Mexico 5‰. Consequently, to compare mortality rates we use the **standardised mortality rate** (SMR) or **age-specific mortality rates** (ASMR), such as the **infant mortality rate** (IMR).

The IMR is defined as the total number of deaths of children aged less than 1 year per 1000 live births. **Life expectancy (E_0)** is the average number of years that a person can be expected to live, given that demographic factors remain unchanged.

At the global scale, the pattern of mortality in the MEDCs differs from that in the LEDCs. In the former, as a consequence of better nutrition, health care and environmental conditions, the death rate falls steadily to a level of about 9‰, with very high life expectancies (over 75 years). In many of the very poorer countries, the high death rates and low life expectancies are still common, although both have shown steady improvement over the past few decades due to improvements in food supply, water, sanitation and housing. This trend, unfortunately, has been reversed as a consequence of AIDS.

As a country develops, the major forms of illness and death change. LEDCs are characterised by a high proportion of infectious/contagious diseases such as cholera, tuberculosis, gastroenteritis and diarrhoea. These may prove fatal. By contrast, in MEDCs, fatal diseases are more likely to be degenerative diseases such as cancer or heart disease. The change in disease pattern from infectious to degenerative is known as the **epidemiological transition model**. (Epidemiology is the study of the incidence of diseases.) Such a change generally took about a 100 years in MEDCs but is taking place faster in LEDCs. At both the global and at a more local scale, variations in mortality rates occur:

- **Age structure**: some populations, such as those in retirement towns and especially in the older industrialised countries, have very high life expectancies and this in turn results in a rise in the CDR. Countries with a large proportion of young people will have much lower death rates (Mexico, with 34% of its population under the age of 15 years, has a CBR of 5‰).
- **Social class**: the poorer people within any population have higher mortality rates than the more affluent and in some countries, such as South Africa, this will also be reflected in racial groups.
- **Occupation**: certain occupations are hazardous – the armed forces, farmers, oil workers and miners, for example. Some diseases are linked to specific occupations – mining and respiratory disease is a good example.

- **Place of residence**: in urban areas mortality rates are higher in areas of relative poverty and deprivation, such as inner cities and shanty towns. This is due to overcrowding, pollution, high population densities and stress. In many rural areas, where there is widespread poverty and limited farm productivity, mortality rates are high. For example, in the rural north-east of Brazil, life expectancy is 27 years shorter than in the richer south-east region.
- **Child mortality and the infant mortality rate (IMR)**: while the CBR shows small fluctuations over time, the IMR can show greater fluctuations and is one of the most sensitive indicators of the level of development. This is due to the following: (a) high IMRs are only found in the poorest countries; and (b) the causes of infant deaths are often preventable. IMRs are low where there is safe water supply and adequate sanitation, housing, health care and nutrition.

In South Africa the IMR varies with race. Whites have a higher income and a better standard of living and have a lower IMR (10–15‰) than the other racial groups (blacks 50–100‰, coloureds 45–55‰).

The cause and age of death also varies with race:

- for whites, **neonatal** (0–7 days) and **perinatal** deaths (7–28 days) are more likely due to congenital (birth) deformities
- for blacks, they are more likely to be due to low birth weight, gastro-enteritis, pneumonia and jaundice, occurring between 7 and 365 days, the **post-neonatal** period.

3 Population Structure

Population structure or **composition** refers to any *measurable* characteristic of the population. This includes the age, sex, ethnicity, language, religion and occupation of the population.

Population pyramids tell us a great deal of information about the age and sex *structure* of a population (Figure 24):

- a wide base indicates a high birth rate
- narrowing base suggests falling birth rate
- straight or near vertical sides reveals low death rate
- concave slopes characterise high death rates
- bulges in the slope suggest high rates of in-migration (for instance, excess males 20–35 years will be economic migrants looking for work; excess elderly, usually female, will indicate retirement resorts)
- deficits in the slope indicate out-migration or age-specific or sex-specific deaths (epidemics, war).

In many parts of the world the population is ageing (Figure 25). This brings a number of problems, as illustrated in Germany.

(a) Oxford

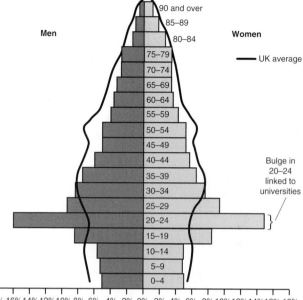

(b) Christchurch

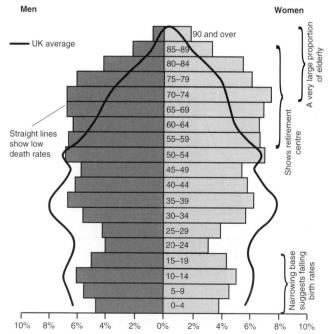

Figure 24 Population pyramid for (a) Oxford, (b) Christchurch, (c) Milton Keynes and (d) London. *Source*: Office of National Statistics

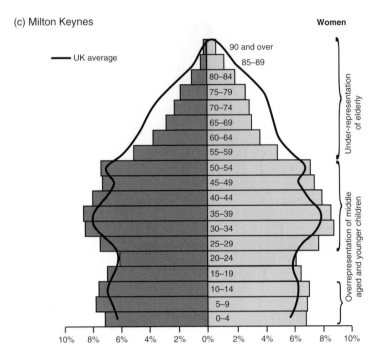

(c) Milton Keynes

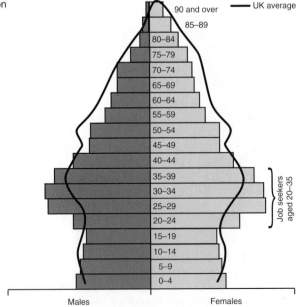

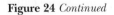

Figure 24 *Continued*

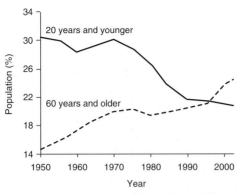

Figure 25 Population of Germany by age. *Source*: German Federal Statistical Office

CASE STUDY: GERMANY'S DECLINING POPULATION

Germany has one of the lowest fertility rates in Europe at 1.36 children (as in 2000) (see Figure 26). While this is mainly due to a predominantly highly educated female population and the choice to have children later in life (on average, children are born to mothers over 30), other reasons for this low rate are attributed to the lack of childcare facilities and childcare

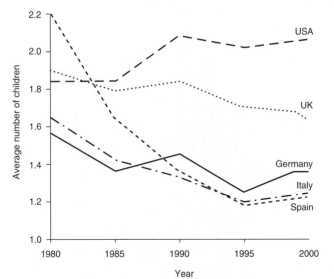

Figure 26 Average number of children per woman of child-bearing age *Source*: OECD, Eurostat

support. To try and rectify this, the government is planning to spend €1.5 billion a year after 2005 on childcare, and to invest €4 billion in all-day schools.

4 Growth Rates

The growth rate is the average annual percentage change in population, resulting from a surplus (or deficit) of births over deaths and the balance of migrants entering and leaving a country. The rate may be positive or negative. Growth rate is a factor in determining how great a burden would be imposed on a country by the changing needs of its people for infrastructure (e.g. schools, hospitals, housing, roads), resources (e.g. food, water, electricity) and jobs.

(a) Doubling Times

The doubling time refers to the length of time it takes for a population to double in size, assuming its natural growth rate remains constant. Approximate values for it can be obtained by calculating the formula: doubling time (years) = (70/growth rate in percentage) (see Figure 27).

Country	Growth rate (%)	Doubling time (years)
Denmark	0.1	700
Brazil	0.9	78
Indonesia	1.6	44
Uganda	3.0	23

Figure 27 Doubling times for selected countries

CASE STUDY: WORLD POPULATION GROWTH

The world's population is growing very rapidly. Most of this growth is quite recent. The world's population doubled between 1650 and 1850, 1850 and 1920, 1920 and 1970. It is thus taking less time for the population to double. Up to 95% of population growth is taking place in less economically developed countries (LEDCs).

The world population increased by 74 million people – the population of Egypt – in 2002, but that is well below the peak of 87 million added in 1989–1990. At 1.2% a year, the increase is also well below the 2.2% annual growth seen 40 years ago. The slowdown in global population growth is linked primarily to declines in fertility (Figure 28).

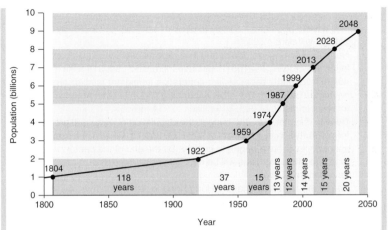

Figure 28 Global population growth. *Source*: UN statistics

In 1990, women, on average, were giving birth to 3.3 children in their lifetime. By 2002 it had dropped to 2.6 children – slightly above the level needed to assure replacement of the population. The level of fertility for the world will probably descend below replacement level before 2050. The projections also suggest that AIDS, which has killed more than 20 million people in the past 20 years, will lower the average life expectancy at birth in some countries to around 30 years of age by 2010. AIDS continues to have its greatest impact in developing countries of Asia, Latin America and especially sub-Saharan Africa. Botswana and South Africa are among countries that may see population decline because of AIDS deaths.

The price to be paid for a shrinking world population is an increase in the number of elderly people. Life expectancy is increasing, but social security systems are not. The forecast divides the world into 13 regions. In all but two – North America and Latin America – the population is predicted to be falling by the end of the century.

The biggest falls are in China, down from 1.4 billion to 1.25 billion in 2100, and in Europe, from 813 million to 607 million. The population in the European part of the former Soviet Union is falling sharply already; it is predicted to shrink by 18 million to 218 million in 2025, and to slump to 141 million, a 40% depopulation, by 2100.

Other regions will have shrinking populations by 2100, but will still have many more people than they do today. Sub-Saharan Africa's population will be 1.5 billion in 2100, compared to 611 million now, and south Asia will by 2100 contain almost two billion people, against 1.4 billion at present (see Figure 29).

- The world's population is likely to peak at nine billion in 2070. By 2100, it will be 8.4 billion
- North America will be one of only two regions in the world with a population still growing in 2100. It will have increased from 314 million to 454 million, partly because first-generation immigrant families tend to have more children. The other expanding region is Latin America – forecast to increase from 515 million to 934 million
- Despite disease, war and hunger, the population of Africa will grow from 784 million to 1.6 billion in 2050. By 2100 it will be 1.8 billion, although it will have begun to decline. By the end of the century more than one-fifth of Africans will be over 60 years, more than in present-day western Europe
- The China region (China and Hong Kong together with five smaller neighbouring nations) will see its population shrink significantly by 2100, from 1.4 billion to 1.25 billion. Because of its education programme, by 2020, when China is reaching its population peak of about 1.6 billion, it will have more well-educated people than Europe and North America combined
- India will overtake China as the world's most populous nation by 2020
- Europe – including Turkey and the former Soviet Union west of the Urals – will see its population fall from 813 million to 607 million in 2100: from 13% of the world's population to just 7%. Eastern countries such as Russia have already seen their populations fall; western Europe's is likely to peak in the next few decades
- One-tenth of the world's population is over 60 years of age. By 2100, that proportion will have risen to one-third
- In 1950, there were thought to be three times as many Europeans as Africans. By 2100, the proportions will be reversed

Figure 29 Key predictions from the global population forecast

CASE STUDY: UK'S POPULATION GROWTH

The UK population will peak at more than 65 million in 2051. But almost all the growth will be among older people and the working-age population will start to decline within the next 20 years, leaving the country increasingly dependent on immigrants to maintain its economic vitality.

To date, immigration is one part of ensuring the continued success of the UK economy and supporting an ageing population.

But this overall picture masks different patterns in the UK. The population of Scotland is expected to decline continuously from five million in 2002 to 4.5 million in 2041. The numbers in Wales and Northern Ireland are projected to peak in 2031 at 3.1 million and 1.8 million, respectively. The number of children under 16 years of age is projected to fall by 7.4% from 11.8 million in 2002 to just below 11 million in 2014.

The number of people of working age is projected to rise by 3.5% from 36.6 million in 2002 to 37.8 million in 2011. Allowing for the planned change in women's state pension age from 60 to 65 between 2010 and 2020, the working-age population will increase further to 39.4 million by 2021 and then start to fall. Unless more people stay in employment after the traditional retirement age, the country will lose about one million workers over the 10 years to 2031.

5 Population Projections and Population Policies

Population projections are estimates of future population size based on current population trends and policies. They are important as governments need them to plan for future services such as health and education, water supplies and housing. Projections take into account birth and death rates, the age structure of a population, migration patterns and government policies.

Population policies refer to official government actions to control the population in some way:

- **pronatalist** policies are those in favour of increasing the birth rate
- **antinatalist** policies attempt to limit the birth rate
- **immigration** policies limit the number or type of person entering a country
- **redistribution** policies, such as new towns, attempt to limit the number of people in one place by attracting them to other, newer areas.

CASE STUDY: ANTINATALIST POLICIES IN CHINA

Almost one-quarter of the world's population lives in China. Although the government used to believe that a large population made the country strong both economically and politically, it now realises that the larger the population the more people there are to feed, clothe and house. This prompted the government to think about family planning – methods of reducing the number of children being born.

To control its population growth in 1979 the Chinese government introduced its infamous one-child policy. This rewarded families that had only one child and penalised those that had more than one. For example, families that had two or more children paid higher taxes, and the parents were prevented from reaching high-level positions in their jobs. Other measures included forced sterilisations and abortions so that families were limited to one child. The sex ratio at birth in China is around 117 boys to 100 girls, compared with the natural rate of 106 to 100. Selective abortion is a major cause, but many baby girls are probably not registered.

Most Chinese families in urban areas have only one child, and the growing middle classes do not discriminate against daughters as much. However, the countryside remains very traditionally focused on male heirs. But the policy is being relaxed. In most provincial rural areas, couples can have two children without penalties. Increasingly, rich farmers are able and willing to pay fines or bribes in order to get permission to have more children; poor families simply take the view that they have nothing much to lose. The one-child policy was relaxed in October 1999. One of the main results of the policy was gender imbalance.

The Chinese government is offering to pay couples a premium for baby girls to counter the gender imbalance created by the one-child policy. The disparity is even bigger in rural areas, 130 to 100. Moreover, there is a resurgence of female infanticide. Girls are hidden from the authorities, or die at a young age through neglect. Even in urban areas, boys are generally preferred because they are regarded as more able than girls to provide for their families, care for elderly relatives and continue the family line.

China now offers welfare incentives to couples with two daughters and has tightened the prohibition on sex-selective abortions. In some areas, couples with two daughters and no sons have been promised an annual payment of £38 once they reach 60 years of age. The money will also be given to families with only one child to discourage couples with a daughter from trying again for a boy.

In parts of Fujian province, local governments have given housing grants of more than £1000 to couples with two girls.

Statistically, the one-child policy has had some success. The authorities say it has prevented well over 300 million births since it was introduced in 1980 and is fulfilling its initial aim of ensuring that China can combat rural poverty and improve standards of living. China's population stood at 1.3 billion in 2003. As the country's economy continues to grow and transform at an unprecedented rate, pressure to relax the policy looks likely to intensify.

It is forecast that there will be a shortage of potential marriage partners, which will lead to some social instability. The preference for a son makes simple economic sense as they are less likely to leave the family home after marrying and, as higher earners than women, are more able to provide for the extended family.

6 Disease

Every year more than 10 million children die of preventable illnesses – this amounts to more than 30,000 a day. More than 500,000 women a year die in pregnancy and childbirth, with such deaths 100 times more likely in sub-Saharan Africa than in high-income OECD countries. Around the world 42 million people are living with HIV/AIDS, 39 million of them in developing countries. Tuberculosis remains (along with AIDS) the leading infectious killer of adults, causing up to two million deaths a year.

More than a billion people in developing countries – one person in five – lack access to safe drinking water, and 2.4 billion lack access to improved sanitation. Diarrhoea is a major killer of young children: in the 1990s it killed more children than all of the people lost to armed conflict since the Second World War. Most affected are poor people in rural areas and slums.

CASE STUDY: HEALTH PROBLEMS FOR AUSTRALIA'S ABORIGINES

The population of Ninga Mia, an Aboriginal shantytown, experience some of the most deprived conditions in Australia. Here, a third of houses lack bathrooms, and even these are often unhygienic. A house for seven or eight people is commonly the size of a bed-sit, and overcrowding and the issues it brings is a very real problem in Ninga Mia. Ninga Mia is not an isolated case however, Aborigines across Australia are experiencing the same low standard of living.

The likelihood of members of the Aboriginal population catching tuberculosis, or meningitis are 10 and seven times higher than non-indigenous Australians. Life expectancy is 20 years less and the infant mortality rate among indigenous populations is four times higher than the rest of the population. Heart disease and diabetes are three and four times more common among the indigenous population. The roots of these problems are extreme poverty, racism and dispossession of land.

(a) Malaria

Malaria kills up to three million people annually, mostly in sub-Sahara Africa and about 500 million more people suffer from the disease. Malaria is widespread in many tropical countries and mosquito-borne diseases such as malaria and yellow fever still infect around 270 million people each year. The cost of malaria is estimated at over £1 billion annually.

As increasing numbers of people travel, they move into areas where malaria is endemic. The disease is affecting new victims because many people are not immune to the disease; mosquitoes are becoming more drug resistant; mosquitoes are spreading into areas previously free of the insect; agricultural schemes are expanding; there is an increase in irrigation schemes; and there is increasing international travel and trade. There are about 2000 cases of malaria in the UK each year, and in 2003 there were 16 deaths.

As yet there is no accepted vaccine. In southern Tanzania up to 80% of the children are infected with the disease by the age of 6 months. There, 4% of children under the age of 5 years die as a result of malaria. Pregnant women, travellers and refugees are also especially vulnerable to the disease. Malaria deaths – concentrated among African children – could be halved to 500,000 by spending another £600 million a year on known prevention and treatment measures.

Conditions for malaria include stagnant water for the mosquitoes to lay eggs and temperatures of over 16°C for the parasite to develop within the mosquito (above 32°C large numbers of the parasites die). Malaria can cause fever, sweating, anaemia and spleen enlargement, and it can be fatal.

There are short-term costs of malaria such as loss of labour and the costs of preventative and curative health care. There are also long-term costs such as a reduction in tourism, flows of trade and foreign investment. Malaria hinders development.

Some scientists from China believe that they have found a cure for malaria, based on the herb sweet wormwood (*Artemesia annua*).

7 Hunger and Malnutrition

The Food and Agriculture Organization (FAO) estimates that 842 million people are undernourished. Three-fifths of them live in the Asia-Pacific region, and one-quarter in sub-Saharan Africa. The food supply in the Democratic Republic of Congo fell by almost 3% a year from 1990 to 2001, to 1566 kilocalories per person per day. The USA's food supply rose over the same period to 3769 kilocalories per person per day.

The proportion of children under 5 years of age in the developing world who are malnourished to the point of stunting fell from 39% in 1990 to 30% in 2000, says the World Health Organization (WHO). By 2005, this figure is projected to fall below 26%.

Such improvements have stemmed largely from swift economic growth in China and, to a lesser extent, India. Most of the world's malnourished children are still in Asia, but on average Chinese people enjoy a third more calories today than they did two decades ago.

Africans are doing less well. One-third of Africa's people are undernourished, a figure that barely changed between the mid-1990s and the turn of the millennium. In central Africa, which has been thrown

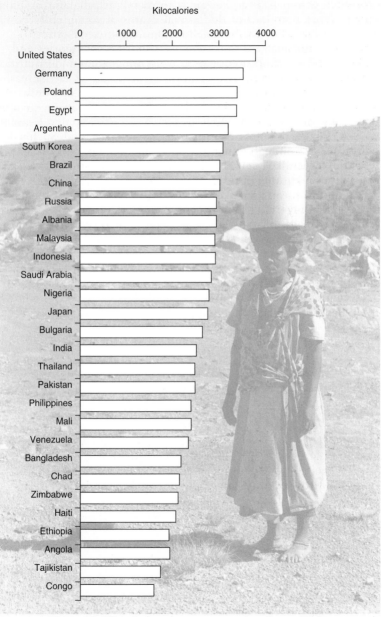

Figure 30 Kilocalories per person per day. *Source*: FAO

into confusion by the war in Congo, the proportion of hungry people rose from 53% to 58% between 1995 and 2001. Underweight infants are much more likely to succumb to diarrhoea, malaria or pneumonia. More than half of the annual deaths of young children are directly or indirectly attributable to malnutrition (see Figure 30).

Hunger and malnutrition refer to a shortage of calories and/or proteins over the short or long term. Most hunger and undernutrition occurs in LEDCs, whereas overnutrition or obesity is an increasing problem in many MEDCs. Malnutrition can be caused by a deficiency of any component of a diet, whether in terms of quality or quantity, that retards normal body functions such as growth and development, or it can be due to illness, causing malabsorption of food. Such a definition is broad enough to include deficiencies of energy calories proteins and minerals as well as the nutritional excesses, which may cause obesity and its related disorders.

Malnutrition can take many forms. Rarely is it outright starvation, more commonly it is a case of specific protein (kwashiorkor) or energy deficiency (marasmus), or a mixture of these (marasmic kwashiorkor) (see Figure 31).

Often it may be manifest only in a seasonal form. In general, a diet that is lacking in one essential food item is likely to be lacking in another.

Although the number of hungry people fell by nearly 20 million in the 1990s, the number of hungry people increased in areas other than

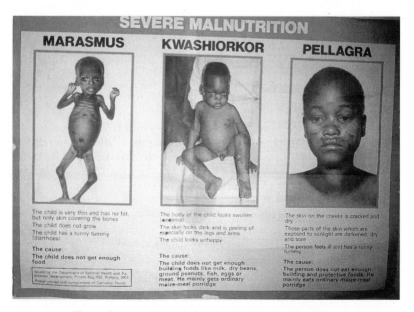

Figure 31 A wallposter showing types of malnutrition

China. South Asia and sub-Saharan Africa are home to the largest concentrations of hungry people. In south Asia the challenge is improving the distribution of food, while in sub-Saharan Africa it involves increasing agricultural productivity.

Many public actions can be used to reduce hunger. Buffer stocks, especially at the local level, can release food into the market during food emergencies – reducing the volatility of prices. Many countries, such as China and India, have such systems. Food stocks can be particularly important for landlocked countries susceptible to droughts.

In addition, many hungry people are landless or lack secure tenure. Agrarian reform is needed to provide rural poor people with secure access to land. Women produce much of the food in sub-Saharan Africa and south Asia yet do not have secure access to land. Low agricultural productivity also needs to be addressed, particularly in marginal ecological regions with poor soils and high climatic variability. The dramatic gains of the **green revolution** have bypassed these areas. Import tariffs protect markets in rich countries and reduce incentives for farmers in poor countries to invest in agriculture, which would contribute to more sustainable food security. Enormous subsidies in rich countries also reduce incentives to invest in long-term food security and depress world market prices – although they can benefit net food importers.

Sen (1984) has analysed major world famines using the concept of entitlements and found that several famines have not been associated with a shortage of food, but rather with a lack of entitlements because the food supply has been withdrawn from certain parts of the country or sections of society, or food prices have risen.

The effects of malnutrition are diverse and interrelated. On the one hand there is the lack of growth in an individual, higher mortality and morbidity rates, and on the other there are indirect effects such as the provision of health-care services, reduced economic output and productivity, lower educational achievements and low incomes.

Malnutrition kills more children in the world than any infectious disease, war or natural disaster, yet it remains a 'silent emergency' arousing little public concern. Malnutrition is implicated in more than six million deaths of children under 5 years each year, more than half of child deaths, and is leaving millions of survivors stunted physically and intellectually.

The persistence of malnutrition has profound and frightening implications for children, society and the future of humankind. Half of the under-5s in south Asia and a third of those in sub-Saharan Africa are malnourished. So too are millions of children, mostly from poor families, in the industrialised world (see Figure 32).

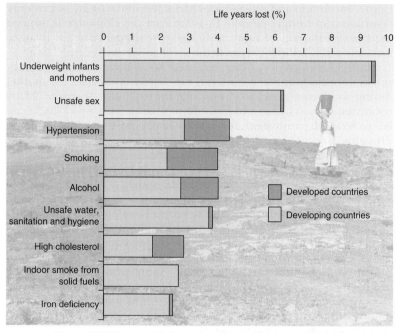

Figure 32 Disease risk factors and contribution to disease.
Source: UN statistics

CASE STUDY: HUNGER IN MSEKENI, MALAWI

Free school lunches provided by the World Food Programme in one of Malawi's poorest regions, Msekeni, have had a great effect. In an area where under-5s are in danger of being stunted due to malnourishment, the opportunity to eat a plate of porridge a day saw the enrolment numbers at the local school double. Instead of being kept at home to work, when education seemed to offer nothing, children are now able to gain their education along with the benefit of being able to eat nutritious food on a regular basis.

(a) Improving Food Quality

Malnutrition is not just caused by not getting enough food, it can also be caused by not getting the right food. Protein energy deficiency is a type of malnutrition and is caused by a diet lacking in the major macronutrients such as carbohydrates, fats and proteins.

A diet lacking in micronutrients is labelled as one of the top 10 risks to health by the World Health Organization. A diet lacking in micronutrients would include a lack of minerals like iodine and iron. A deficiency in either of these can have long-lasting effects. Around 20 million children are born each year with mental disabilities due to a deficiency of iodine in their mothers. The World Food Programme states that an iron deficiency can lead to a decline in productivity through lethargy and fatigue among the workforce and therefore undermine the country's economy by cutting GDP by up to 2% in some cases.

There are a number of short-term solutions that can be employed, like providing people with iodised salt and fortifying flour with iron, but it is a long-term problem and one that will take long-term solutions like education to eradicate it.

8 Food Supply

(a) Global Imbalance in Production and Distribution of Food

There is a global imbalance in the availability of food. This is related to economic development as well as access to guaranteed markets, capital and technology, and government intervention.

In LEDCs there has been a decrease in **production per head** in many countries. Reasons include:

- deteriorating environmental conditions
- poor farming practises
- overpopulation
- underpopulation, as in Rwanda where there were not enough people to harvest crops from the fields
- the neglect of the agricultural sector by the government.

(b) The Green Revolution/High External Input Agriculture

The **green revolution** is the application of science and technology to increase food output. Despite predictions from as long ago as 1798 by Thomas Malthus – that the world's population growth would outstrip the ability of the world to feed its population – this forecast has, thankfully, not come true. This is in part due to what is commonly referred to as the green revolution.

Although at a global level the production of food has surpassed population growth, at a disaggregated level the picture is not always so encouraging. The twentieth century saw several major famines in Asia and Africa, although more often than not it was war or political turmoil that was the cause rather than the result of famine. During the Cold War the two ideologies of capitalism and socialism fought for the allegiance of many LEDCs, each promising release from poverty and hunger by following their respective political economic models.

The solutions to these problems were seen differently by the two sides. The socialist camp thought that abolition of landlordism and its replacement by collective farming would solve food problems – as enforced in China. Other states believed in the redistribution of land to poor people, although not outright collectivisation of land. The capitalist MEDCs sought to promote growth in agricultural productivity and hence rural incomes by technical means, namely the green revolution. This was championed by Dr Norman Borlaug.

Borlaug was a plant breeder who used hybridisation to produce a new variety of wheat with stable and desirable traits. The main strategy adopted was to breed new dwarf varieties that were responsive to artificial fertiliser, particularly nitrogen. The short height of the plants had two advantages: with less leverage from the head acting on the stem, the head could be heavier without causing the stem to bend over and fail, therefore allowing the use of higher doses of fertiliser, and proportionately more of the plant mass would be in grain. However, engineered species had a heightened susceptibility to disease and pests in the early new varieties, so increased use of pesticides and fungicides became part of the revolution. The use of machines resulted in the canopy height being kept constant – this created a micro-climate better suited to disease transmission between plant heads, which were closer together.

Thus, the green revolution required considerable expenditure and was, in a sense, not so well adapted to local environments. The more recent name for this agriculture – high external input agriculture – is perhaps more accurate than the ideological term 'the green revolution' that was applied to it from the 1960s to the 1990s.

Wheat production in Mexico multiplied threefold in the time that Borlaug worked with the Mexican government; and 'dwarf' wheat imported in the mid-1960s was responsible for a massive increase in wheat harvests in Pakistan and India. In 1961 wheat production in India was 11 million tonnes, and in 1991 it was 55 million tonnes. From 1967 to 1990 average wheat yields increased by 3.14% compound annually.

(c) Social and Environmental Effects

Socially, the new technology proved divisive, as in the early days the costs of investment meant the new technology was better suited to bigger and richer farms. Share croppers and others in limited tenancy were evicted as potential profits grew. Environmentally the costs included:

- the loss of indigenous varieties (particularly of wheat)
- a purported addiction of some soils to fertiliser, which means that increasing doses have to be applied
- persistent pesticides in the environment, which are particularly harmful where rice and fish are cultivated together
- a reduced output of straw, which means that animal fodder has to be found from new sources

- rising water tables in some areas, which cause salinisation of the soil if they reach the surface, and a rapid fall in the water table in other areas that are over-pumped. This again is more likely to impact on poor people, who use traditionally dug open wells, than the rich, who have tube wells drilled in their land.

The green revolution provided an increase in agricultural production that undoubtedly has given many governments a breathing space. Although rates of population increase continue to fall, absolute numbers will continue to increase as young populations achieve adulthood and reproduce. By 2050 India and China alone will have added another 800 million people – or an increment equal to three times the population of the USA.

Technological optimists believe that the age of biotechnology and genetic modification will solve these problems. The pessimists fear that the rewards will go to the big corporations, and that the small and poor of LEDCs will be passed by, or forced to pay excessive prices for the new seeds that will undoubtedly be needed.

(d) Food Security

The concept of food security has been central in developing policies to end hunger and malnutrition over the past 25 years. The reason most people are hungry is not because enough food cannot be produced, but because it does not get distributed fairly and because some people are too poor to buy it. Increasing per capita food production alone is not enough to reduce hunger and malnutrition.

(e) Evolution of the Concept

During the 1974 World Food Conference, food security was invoked largely at a national level with an emphasis on maintaining a network of sufficient food reserves to meet a country's food needs. Many LEDCs were quick to identify with this approach, but tended to link it to national goals of food self-sufficiency. In this way, it was reasoned, they would be less dependent on food imports or food aid from MEDCs.

(f) Household Food Security

Poverty is both a symptom and a cause of food insecurity. Increasing the capacity of poor households to purchase food, in addition to what they might be able to grow, is widely viewed as key to enhancing household food security. The majority of the world's poor people live in rural areas, and many of them on marginal lands where they face considerable constraints in producing sufficient food.

Intra-household distribution tends to be biased against women and children, for example in south Asia, which has the largest number of poor and hungry people in the world.

(g) Transitory and Chronic Food Insecurity

Food insecurity can be transitory and chronic. During seasonal fluctuations in food production, or in times of crisis, impoverished households that are experiencing transitory food insecurity may be pushed into a state of chronic food insecurity. At such times, women and young children especially may be at greater risk than others (see Figure 33).

(h) Achieving Food Security

Efforts to increase food security will need to be focused on south Asia and sub-Saharan Africa where more than 50% of the world's poor and hungry live, and where more than 75% of the world's malnourished children will live in the year 2020. Very few countries in the world today have experienced significant economic growth without a solid foundation of agriculture.

In order to feed the population by the year 2020, a 40% increase in grain production is required in the next 20 years. However, more than half of the land area is already used for crop production and pasture.

Types of condition or event	Types of population at risk
Drought	Smallholders with limited resources and non-diversified income
Crop production risks	Small holders on marginal lands
	Landless farm labourers
Disruptions in imports/exports	Small holders heavily dependent on export crops
Falling prices of agricultural exports	Poor households heavily dependent on imported food
Unemployment	Wage-earning households
	Informal-sector employees
Lack of healthcare and sanitation	Entire communities
Poor infrastructure	Poor households
	Vulnerable members (women and children) of households
Political crisis	Households in areas of civil unrest
Government failure	Marginalised ethnic groups

Figure 33 Sources of food and nutrition insecurity

(i) Regenerating Agriculture

All commentators agree that food production will have to increase, and that this will have to come from existing farmland. Sustainable agriculture is defined as agricultural technologies and practices that maximise the productivity of the land while seeking to minimise damage both to valued natural assets (soils, water, air and biodiversity) and to human health (farmers and other rural people, and consumers).

It does this by integrating natural processes such as nutrient cycling, nitrogen fixation, soil regeneration and natural enemies of pests into food production processes. It also seeks to minimise the use of non-renewable inputs (pesticides and fertilisers) that damage the environment or harm the health of farmers and consumers. It makes better use of the knowledge and skills of farmers, so improving their self-reliance.

Sustainable agriculture is multifunctional within landscapes and economies – it produces food and other goods for farm families and markets, but it also contributes to a range of public goods, such as clean water, wildlife and carbon sequestration in soils.

Chapter Summary

- The crude birth rate is a very simple statistic, and comparisons made with it are limited.
- Fertility – and age-specific rates – are preferable.
- The status of women in many countries is low – in Arab countries and in China where the one-child policy has increased the difference in the male-to-female ratio.
- Increasingly, governments play an important role in family planning.
- The crude death rate is a simple statistic.
- The age-structure of the population has an important effect on the country. In MEDCs ageing populations are especially demanding on the economy.
- Although the world's population growth is slowing, it is still growing.
- Diseases are related to poverty and level of development.
- Although there is plenty of food in the world, hunger and malnutrition are widespread.
- The effects of malnutrition are physical, social, economic and emotional.
- There are many ways in which malnutrition can be tackled.
- Globally there are many examples of the successes of food production.
- Food security is one of the big issues of the twenty-first century.
- The green revolution is not the same as food security.

Questions

1. Suggest reasons why world population growth is slowing down.
2. Describe and explain the impact of malaria. Use real-life examples to support your comments.
3. What are the causes and consequences of malnutrition?
4. Define the term 'food security'. What are the factors that promote food insecurity?

4 Settlement and Development

1 Urbanisation

In 1800 only 2% of the world's population was urban. However, by 1950 this figure had increased to 30%, and by 2000 it was 47%. Moreover, more than half of the world's population will be living in urban areas by 2008, and by 2030 it is expected to be 60%. Rapid urbanisation is one of the principal characteristics of LEDCs (Figure 34).

(a) Urbanisation in LEDCs

More than two-thirds of the world's urban population is now in Africa, Asia, Latin America and the Caribbean. The population in urban areas in LEDCs will grow from 1.9 billion in 2000 to 3.9 billion in 2030. In MEDCs, however, the urban population is expected to increase very slowly, from 0.9 billion in 2000 to one billion in 2030.

The overall population growth rate for the world for that period is 1%, while the growth rate for urban areas is nearly double, or 1.8%. At this rate, the world's urban population will double in 38 years. Growth will be even more rapid in the urban areas of LEDCs, averaging 2.3% per year, with a doubling time of 30 years.

The urbanisation process in MEDCs has stabilised with about 75% of the population living in urban areas. Latin America and the Caribbean were 50% urbanised by 1960 but are now in the region of

Region	1950	1980	2010*
Urban population (millions of inhabitants)			
Africa	33	130	458
Asia	244	706	1816
Latin America and the Caribbean	69	233	463
Rest of the world	404	685	849
Percentage of population living in urban areas			
Africa	14.6	27.3	43.6
Asia	17.4	26.7	43.6
Latin America and the Caribbean	41.4	64.9	78.6
Rest of the world	55.3	70.5	78
Proportion of the world's urban population living in			
Africa	4.4	7.4	12.8
Asia	32.5	40.3	50.6
Latin America and the Caribbean	9.2	13.3	12.9
Rest of the World	53.9	39	23.7

Figure 34 Trends and projections in urban populations
by region, 1950–2010. *Projected

75%. Although Africa is predominantly rural, with only 37.3% living in urban areas in 1999, with a growth rate of 4.87%, Africa is the continent with the fastest rate of urbanisation. By 2030 Asia and Africa will both have higher numbers of urban dwellers than any other major area of the world. Two aspects of this rapid growth have been the increase in the number of large cities and the historically unprecedented size of the largest cities.

CASE STUDY: URBANISATION IN CHINA

Shanghai is a city of 20 million residents, which is 1.6% of the Chinese population, but it attracts 10% of all foreign investment and creates 5% of GDP. The relaxation of restrictions on labour migrants has seen a large influx of rural migrants into the cities. Of the 20-million-strong population in Shanghai, only 13.5 million are considered to be permanent residents. The rest are considered to be part of the floating population, many are migrant workers attracted by the booming construction industry and high wages. Shanghai has seen an increase in population of three million people looking for work. The government is planning to move even more people from rural areas into the city over the coming years, but this will create pressure on space and infrastructure. Soaring house prices and traffic congestion and pollution are all problems that will only be exacerbated by the increase in migrants.

2 Megacities and World Cities

A megacity is a city with over 10 million people. In 1950 there was only one megacity – New York. In 2000 there were 22 cities with a population of between five and 10 million; there were 402 cities with a population of between one and five million; and 433 cities in the half to one million category. By 2015 it is expected that there will be 23 cities with a population over 10 million. Of the 23 cities expected to reach 10 million plus by 2015, 19 of them will be in LEDCs (see Figure 35).

Most of the world's megacities had slower population growth rates during the 1980s and 1990s. Many of the larger cities are significantly smaller than had been expected. For instance, Mexico City had around 18 million people in 2000 – not the 31 million predicted in 1980. Kolkata (Calcutta) has fewer than 13 million inhabitants in 2000, not the 40–50 million people predicted in the 1970s.

A range of factors help to explain this. First, in many LEDC cities, slow economic growth (or economic decline) attracted fewer people. Second, the capacity of cities outside the very large metropolitan centres to attract a significant proportion of new investment was limited. Third, lower rates of natural increase have occurred, as fertility rates come down.

1950		1975		2000		2015	
1. New York	12.3	1. Tokyo	19.8	1. Tokyo	26.4	1. Tokyo	26.4
		2. New York	15.9	2. Mexico City	18.1	2. Mumbai	26.1
		3. Shanghai	11.4	3. Mumbai	18.1	3. Lagos	23.2
		4. Mexico City	11.2	4. São Paulo	17.8	4. Dhaka	21.1
		5. São Paulo	10.0	5. New York	16.6	5. São Paulo	20.4
				6. Lagos	13.4	6. Karachi	19.2
				7. Los Angeles	13.1	7. Mexico City	19.2
				8. Kolkata	12.9	8. New York	17.4
				9. Shanghai	12.9	9. Jakarta	17.3
				10. Buenos Aires	12.6	10. Kolkata	17.3
				11. Dhaka	12.3	11. Delhi	16.8
				12. Karachi	11.8	12. Metro Manila	14.8
				13. Delhi	11.7	13. Shanghai	14.6
				14. Jakarta	11.0	14. Los Angeles	14.1
				15. Osaka	11.0	15. Buenos Aires	14.1
				16. Metro Manila	10.9	16. Cairo	13.8
				17. Beijing	10.8	17. Istanbul	12.5
				18. Rio de Janeiro	10.6	18. Beijing	12.3
				19. Cairo	10.6	19. Rio de Janeiro	11.9
						20. Osaka	11.0
						21. Tianjin	10.7
						22. Hyderabad	10.5
						23. Bangkok	10.1

Figure 35 The world's megacities, 1950–2015; figures are population in millions

However, there were some large cities whose population growth rates remained high during the 1980s – for instance, Dhaka (Bangladesh) and many cities in India and China, and strong economic performance by such cities is the most important factor in explaining this.

Given the association between economic growth and urbanisation, a steady increase in the level of urbanisation in low-income nations is only likely to take place if they also have steadily growing economies.

3 World Cities and Development

Certain cities have become the key locations for international capitalism. **World cities** serve to integrate regional, national and international economies into a global economic system. The functions of world cities are directly reflected in the structure and dynamics of their employment. World cities are points of destination for large numbers of both domestic and/or international migrants.

World cities create spatial and class inequalities (giving rise to cores and peripheries and semi-peripheries at the global scale, and developed and less-developed regions at the national scale). World-city growth generates social costs (e.g. those that come from the rapid influx of poor workers into these cities and the massive needs for housing, education and health that this generates) for which governments cannot cater.

While most of the primary world cities, such as London, Paris, New York, and Tokyo, are located in the 'core' countries of the MEDC, Singapore and São Paulo are recognised as primary world cities in the semi-periphery. In addition, Hong Kong, Bangkok, Manila, Rio de Janeiro, and Johannesburg are recognised as part of an emerging network of secondary world cities in LEDCs (Figure 36). In short, world cities may be seen as points of accumulation in a TNC-dominated capitalist global system.

In the modern world, large cities are the principal adopters of innovations, so that natural growth poles become evermore associated with the upper level of the urban system.

(a) The Challenge of Slums

Efforts to improve the living conditions of slum dwellers (especially within LEDCs) peaked during the 1980s. However, renewed concern about poverty has recently led governments to adopt a specific target on slums in the United Nations Millennium Declaration, which aims to significantly improve the lives of at least 100 million slum dwellers by 2020.

The total number of slum dwellers in the world stood at about 924 million people in 2001. This represents about 32% of the world's total urban population (Figure 37). At that time, 43% of the combined urban populations of all developing regions lived in slums, while 78.2% of the urban population in LEDCs were slum dwellers (Figure 38). In some

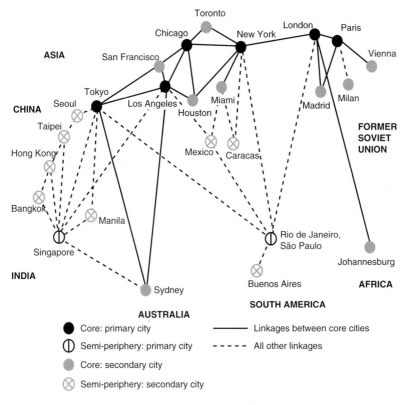

Figure 36 World cities

LEDC cities, slums are so pervasive that it is the rich who have to seg-
regate themselves behind gated enclaves.

There are negative and positive aspects of slums (Figure 40). On the
negative side, slums have the most intolerable of urban housing conditions, which frequently include:

- insecurity of tenure
- lack of basic services, especially water and sanitation (Figure 39a)
  especially in slums (Figure 39b)
- inadequate and, sometimes, unsafe building structures
- overcrowding
- location on hazardous land
- high concentrations of poverty and of social and economic deprivation, which may include broken families, unemployment, and economic, physical and social exclusion
- slum dwellers have limited access to credit and formal job markets
  due to stigmatisation, discrimination and geographic isolation

Major area, region	Total population (millions)	Urban population (millions)	Percentage urban population	Estimated slum population	
				(%)	(thousands)
World	6134	2923	47.7	31.6	923,986
Developed regions	1194	902	75.5	6.0	54,068
Europe	726	534	73.6	6.2	33,062
Other	467	367	78.6	5.7	21,006
Developing regions	4940	2022	40.9	43.0	869,918
Northern Africa	146	76	52.0	28.2	21,355
Sub-Saharan Africa	667	231	34.6	71.9	166,208
Latin America and Caribbean	527	399	75.8	31.9	127,567
Eastern Asia	1364	533	39.1	46.4	193,824
South-central Asia	1507	452	30.0	58.8	262,354
South-eastern Asia	530	203	38.3	28.0	56,781
Western Asia	192	125	64.9	33.1	41,331
Oceania	8	2	26.7	24.1	499
Least developed countries (LDCs)	685	179	26.2	78.2	140,114
Landlocked developing countries (LLDCs)	275	84	30.4	56.5	47,303
Small island developing states (SIDS)	52	30	57.9	24.4	7321

Figure 37 Total, urban and estimated slum population by major region, 2001. *Sources*: United Nations Population Division, UN-Habitat

- slums are often recipients of the city's nuisances, including industrial effluent and noxious waste, and the only land accessible to slum dwellers is often fragile, dangerous or polluted – land that no one else wants
- people in slum areas suffer inordinately from water-borne diseases such as typhoid and cholera, as well as more opportunistic ones that accompany HIV/AIDS.

Slum-dwelling women – and the children they support – are the greatest victims of all. Slum areas are also commonly believed to be places with a high incidence of crime, although this is not universally true since slums with strong social control systems will often have low crime rates.

On the positive side, slums are:

- the first stopping point for immigrants – they provide the low-cost and only affordable housing that will enable the immigrants to save for their eventual absorption into urban society
- the place of residence for low-income employees, slums keep the wheels of the city turning in many different ways

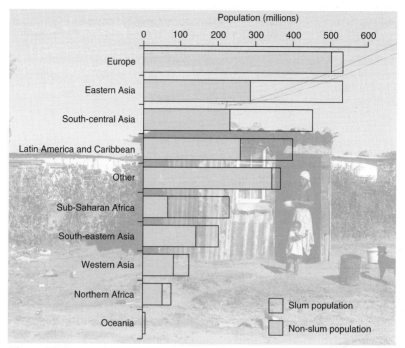

Figure 38 Proportion of slum dwellers in urban population by region, 2001.
Source: UN-Habitat

- many informal entrepreneurs operating from slums have clienteles extending to the rest of the city
- most slum dwellers are people struggling to make an honest living, within the context of extensive urban poverty and formal unemployment
- slums are also places in which the vibrant mixing of different cultures frequently results in new forms of artistic expression.

Many past responses to the problem of urban slums have been based on the belief that provision of improved housing and related services (through slum upgrading) and physical eradication of slums will, on their own, solve the slum problem (see the Case Study on Nairobi, page 71). Solutions based on this premise have failed to address the main underlying causes of slums, of which poverty is the most significant. Future policies must support the livelihoods of the urban poor by enabling urban informal-sector activities to flourish and develop, by linking low-income housing development to income generation, and by ensuring easy geographical access to jobs through pro-poor transport and more appropriate location of low-income settlements. Slum policies should be integrated within broader, people-focused urban poverty reduction policies that address the various dimensions of poverty. Participatory slum upgrading programmes that include urban poverty reduction objectives is the current best practice.

Region	Water connection	Sewerage	Electricity	Telephone	Access to water
Sub-Saharan Africa	48.4	30.9	53.9	15.5	73.5
North Africa and Middle East	79.1	65.9	91.8	42.0	88.0
Asia and the Pacific	65.9	58.0	94.4	57.1	94.8
Latin America and Caribbean	83.7	63.5	91.2	51.7	89.1
All developing countries	75.8	64.0	86.5	52.1	88.9

Figure 39a Connections to infrastructure (%). *Notes*: 'Water connection' refers to the percentage of households with a piped water connection. 'Access to water' means having potable water within 200 metres of the household (e.g. standpipes, wells, etc.), and includes water connections (since most countries presume piped water is potable)

Region	Water	Sewerage	Electricity	Telephone	Access to water
Sub-Saharan Africa	19.1	7.4	20.3	2.9	40.0
North Africa and Middle East	35.7	21.5	35.9	30.0	42.7
Asia and the Pacific	38.3	7.4	75.7	25.4	89.1
Latin America and Caribbean	57.9	30.3	84.7	32.0	66.8
All developing countries	37.2	19.8	59.1	25.4	57.6

Figure 39b Connections to infrastructure – informal settlements (%). (These data may contain inaccuracies as sample sizes are small and measurement is uncertain)

The locus of poverty is moving from the countryside to cities, in a process now recognised as the 'urbanisation of poverty'. The absolute number of poor and undernourished in urban areas is increasing, as are the numbers of urban poor who suffer from malnutrition.

While traditional approaches to the slum problem have tended to concentrate on improvement of housing, infrastructure and physical environmental conditions, a more comprehensive approach to addressing the issue of employment for slum dwellers and the urban poor in general is needed. Slums are largely a manifestation of urban poverty. Thus, future policies must go beyond the physical dimension of slums by addressing the problems that underlie urban poverty.

Slum policies should be integrated with broader, people-focused urban poverty reduction policies that deal with the varied aspects of poverty, including employment and incomes, shelter, food, health, education, and access to basic urban infrastructure and services (Figure

- A total of 923,986,000 people, or 31.6% of the world's total urban population, live in slums; 43% of the urban population of all developing regions combined live in slums; 78.2% of the urban population in the LEDCs live in slums.
- The total number of slum dwellers in the world increased by about 36% during the 1990s and, in the next 30 years, the global number of slum dwellers will increase to about two billion if no concerted action to address the challenge of slums is taken.
- More than 41% of Kolkata's slum households have lived in slums for more than 30 years; more than 70% of the households have lived in slums for more than 15 years; 16% of the population has been living in slums for 6–15 years; and new entrants into slums, with duration of stay of up to 5 years, constitute only 4% of the slum population.
- In most African cities between 40% and 70% of the city's population lives in slums or squatter settlements. Many African cities are doubling their population within two decades. In a city like Nairobi, 60% of the population lives in slums that occupy about 5% of the land.
- While most slum dwellers are dependent on the informal sector for their livelihoods, slum populations in many parts of the world (e.g. in Pune, India and Ibadan, Nigeria) quite often include university lecturers, university students, government civil servants and formal private sector employees.
- About one out of every four LEDC countries has a constitution or national laws that contain clauses that impede women owning land and taking mortgages in their own names; women (and the children that they care for) are the worst victims of infectious diseases in slums; in some African cities, slums are a refuge for women who are fleeing difficult situations created by divorce or marriage and property inheritance disputes.
- All slum households in Bangkok have a colour television; the average number of TVs per household is 1.6; almost all of the households have a refrigerator; two-thirds of the households have a washing machine and, on average, 1.5 mobile phones.
- Singapore is one of the few countries that successfully practices comprehensive public sector housing development, with housing policies and institutions advancing systematically and comprehensively with the economy; 82% of Singapore's current housing stock has been built by the Housing Development Board (HDB); an average of 9% of gross domestic product (GDP) per year has been allocated for housing, compared with around 4% in Organization for Economic Co-operation and Development (OECD) countries.
- The Orangi Pilot Project in Karachi, Pakistan, where residents constructed sewers to 72,000 dwellings over 12 years from 1980 to 1992, contributing more than $2 million from their own resources, now includes basic health, family planning, and education and empowerment components, is considered to be one of the most successful illustrations of the current best practice of participatory slum upgrading.

Figure 40 Slum factfile

41). Improving incomes and jobs for slum dwellers, however, requires robust national economic growth. Current evidence suggests that globalisation in its present form has not always worked in favour of the urban poor and has, in fact, exacerbated their social and economic exclusion in some countries.

Environmental
Atmospheric pollution from a variety of sources, especially from industrial, domestic and transport services
Traffic congestion – moving the daily flow of commuters
Sewage and waste disposal
Water pollution
Rapid urban sprawl, causing loss of land and creating wide areas of slums
Dereliction
Flooding or landslides affecting especially poor people who cannot choose to live in safe locations

Socio-cultural
Zones of poverty within the city can become areas of high crime and social deprivation
Ghettoisation of low-income and ethnic groups leading to friction between groups
Creation of an urban underclass with limited powers to improve their quality of life and health

Economic
Providing resources for the large numbers of new arrivals
Services such as health, education, housing, employment, water and sewerage are increasingly costly to provide

Political
The difficulties of governing cities effectively to cope with the range of problems; declining incomes from rates

Figure 41 Urban challenges

(b) Investment in Infrastructure

At the core of efforts to improve slum environments and enhance economically productive activities is the need to invest in infrastructure – to provide water and sanitation, electricity, access roads, footpaths and waste management. Low-income housing and slum-upgrading policies need to pay attention to the financing of citywide infrastructure development.

Upgrading existing slums is more effective than resettling slum dwellers and should become the normal practice in future slum initiatives. The eradication of slums and resettlement of slum dwellers can create more problems than are solved. Eradication and relocation unnecessarily destroy a large stock of housing affordable to the urban poor and the new housing provided has frequently turned out to be unaffordable, with the result that relocated households move back into slum accommodation.

CASE STUDY: SLUM CLEARANCE IN KENYA

The Nairobi government is in the midst of clawing back land designated for road building or land next to railway lines, which was illegally developed into slum areas by landlords under the leadership of President Daniel arap Moi.

However, this policy to reclaim public land is impacting on the poorest of Nairobi's population, those that live in the slums.

Over 300,000 people face eviction from their homes. The government is making some moves to re-house people, but the estates planned for the populations in the Kibera slum are not enough to house all of the slum dwellers. In areas, there are estimated to be 80,000 inhabitants per square kilometre, and that compares to 360 in a more affluent area. This is an ever-growing problem as rural migrants seek work in urban areas.

CASE STUDY: RIO DE JANEIRO

The history of Rio's slums is one of industrial and infrastructural development, high fertility rates and urbanisation that persistently led to the displacement of the urban poor.

Rio became the political and economic centre of Brazil in the 1700s with the gold boom, but it was in the twentieth century that industrial growth resulted in a rapid increase in population and a spreading outwards. By 2000 it had a population of 10.6 million people.

The expansion particularly in the outer urban and suburban areas, resulted primarily from in-migration of rural dwellers, by natural increase and also from the decentralisation of lower income residents from the centre or suburbs of Rio. The consequence of this change has been the concentration of some of the poorest groups of the population in these zones. The distribution of population reveals a concentric pattern of wealth differences, generally coinciding with the four functional zones of the city:

- centre (*nucleo*) – the historic core of the city that includes the CBD, the high-class residential areas and the industrial port complexes, where the city's main functions are located
- the inner urban area (*zona imediata*) – older suburbs with a good infrastructure, and a mix of traditional and modern industry
- the outer urban area (*zona intermediata*) – the newer outer fringes of the expanding urban area, including Nova Iguacu and Duque de Caxias, which are industrial cities in their own right
- the rural–urban fringe (*zona distante*) – a less urbanised zone beyond the commuting zone of Rio.

Social Segregation

Wide inequalities of wealth and of the provision of urban services are evident. The core and suburban areas show a concentration of wealth, high-quality accommodation, the provision of municipal services, access to the central business district (CBD) and the

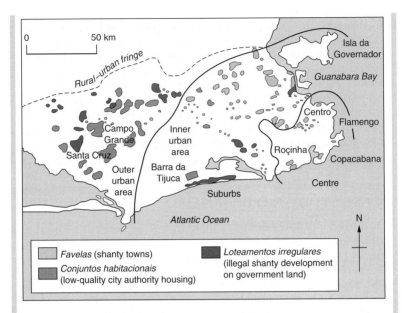

Figure 42 Location of *favelas*

popular beachfronts, while the city's margins are poorly provided with basic services, transport and electricity networks. The even poorer informal squatter settlements (***favelas***) are also found outside the urban area, or interspersed in the central area on land that is unsuitable for development, such as steep hill slopes (Figure 42).

Barra da Tijuca represents the most recent example of the decentralisation of the rich, containing many attractions for Rio's expanding middle and higher income groups with its pleasant environment of mountain views, forest, lagoons and 20 km of beaches. It is an area four times larger than the increasingly congested and polluted central zone, but still only 30 minutes away by motorway. The area expanded from 2500 inhabitants in 1960 to 98,000 in 1991. Accommodation consists of low-rise residential areas interspersed with clusters of high-rise apartments, centred on two commercial cores with shopping malls and hypermarkets. The settlement reflects a motorised, consumer-orientated and wealth-accumulating life style.

By contrast, inland is the area of Jacarepagua, containing low-quality housing estates (*conjuntos habitacionais*), which suffer from remoteness, a lack of public transport and of services, and poor maintenance.

The rise of the *favelas* as an urban feature of Rio has been rapid. The official definition of such settlements are residential areas lacking formal organisation or basic services, containing 60 or more families who are squatting illegally on the site. In 1992 just under one million people (nearly 20% of the total population) lived in 765 *favelas* of varying sizes. The largest has an estimated total population of 80,000. Initially their destruction and the removal of the residents to *conjuntos habitacionais* in the suburbs was the significant policy. The clearance of *favela* sites for the building of high-class apartment blocks and condominiums served to maintain the status and value of the central area. In 1990 a programme of electrification was started, as a means of improving conditions in the *favelas*. While long-established *favelas*, some dating back to 1940, have a mix of commercial services serving a more diverse socio-economic population, the worst conditions are still found in the most recent *favelas* where there is a complete absence of basic services, low incomes and high unemployment.

4 Quality of Life and Deprivation

Within most cities there is considerable variation in the quality of life. This raises questions about equality of opportunity and social justice. In MEDCs and LEDCs there are areas that are labelled as 'poor', and these are zones of deprivation, poverty, and exclusion. In MEDCs it is often inner city areas or ghettos, whereas in LEDCs it is frequently shanty towns, that exhibit the worst conditions. The factors associated with deprivation are varied but they result in a cycle of urban deprivation and a poor quality of life.

(a) Measuring Deprivation

There are a number of indices used to measure deprivation. These include:

- physical measures – such as quality of housing, levels of pollution, vandalism, graffiti
- social indicators – including crime (reported and fear of), levels of health and access to health care, standards of education, proportion of population on subsidised benefits (unemployment, incidence of crime, disability, free school meals), proportion of lone-parent families
- economic indices – access to employment, unemployment and underemployment; levels of income
- political measures – opportunities to vote and to take part in community organisation.

On the basis of the index, 14 out of the 20 most deprived districts in England are in London. The most deprived boroughs in London are in inner-city areas, especially in the east, such as Newham. By contrast, the most affluent districts are in the outer suburbs such as Bromley. There are similar problems in France.

CASE STUDY: FRANCE'S SLUM ESTATES

The 751 sink estates, or *quartiers sensibles*, identified in France are to be the focus of a programme to either rebuild or renovate 400,000 council flats. Roads, public buildings, benches and lighting will also be addressed. The flats were built in the 1950s, 1960s and 1970s to house immigrant workers, but little work has been carried out on the upkeep of them since that time and the problems cannot be ignored any longer. So the French government is to spend £21 billion over 5 years to clean up 163 of the identified estates.

The areas have become ghettos with up to 50% of the population, many of them second-generation immigrants, living there unemployed. Petit Bard is an example of such an estate.

5 The Housing Crisis in LEDCs

Provision of enough quality housing is also a major problem in LEDCs. There are at least four aspects to the management of housing stock: quality of housing – with proper water, sanitation, electricity and space; quantity of housing – having enough units to meet demand; availability and affordability of housing; and housing tenure (ownership or rental).

There are a variety of possible solutions to the housing problem: new towns; government support for low-income self-built housing; subsidies for home building; flexible loans to help shanty-town dwellers; slum upgrading in central areas; improved private and public rental housing; support for the informal sector/small businesses operating at home; site and service schemes; encouragement of community schemes; and construction of health and educational services.

(a) Housing the Urban Poor

There is no simple way of defining precisely a housing problem. What constitutes poor housing is not just about physical standards. There is little point providing a poor family with a fully serviced, three-bedroom house if the family cannot afford the rent or mortgage repayments.

In general, homelessness is a major problem in relatively few LEDC cities. According to the World Bank only 0.8% of Africans, 0.4% of East Asians and 0.6% of Latin Americans 'sleep outside dwelling units or in temporary shelter in charitable institutions'. It is only in south Asia that homelessness seems to be a significant issue, with 7.8% of the population living on the streets. Beyond the Indian sub-continent, most people in LEDC cities have homes.

Most urban governments are concerned about illegality: when land has been stolen, when green areas have been invaded or when basic building standards are ignored. Many Third World governments consider that a key ingredient in housing improvements is to make ownership available to all.

LEDC governments would not be able to solve their housing problems even if they were to try. The best that they could be expected to do in an environment of general poverty is to improve living conditions. They should try to:

- reduce numbers of people living at average densities of more than 1.5 persons in each room
- increase access to electricity and potable water
- improve sanitary facilities
- prevent families moving into areas that are physically unsafe
- encourage households to improve the quality of their accommodation.

A sensible approach is to destroy slums as seldom as possible, on the grounds that every displaced family needs to be rehoused and removing families is often disastrous. Governments should also avoid building formal housing for the very poor. Sensible governments will attempt to upgrade inadequate accommodation by providing it with infrastructure and services of an appropriate standard.

There are no easy solutions to Third World housing problems because poor housing is merely one manifestation of generalised poverty. Decent shelter can never be provided while there is widespread poverty.

(b) Urban Agriculture

The phrase 'urban agriculture' initially sounds like a contradiction in terms; however, the phenomenon has grown in significance in the cities of LEDCs over the past 20 years. Evidence suggests that in some cities urban agriculture may already occupy up to 35% of the land area, may employ up to 36% of the population and may supply up to 50% of urban fresh vegetable needs.

Advantages	Concerns
Vital or useful supplement to food procurement strategies	Conflict over water supply, particularly in arid or semi-arid areas
Various environmental benefits	Health concerns, particularly from use of contaminated wastes
Employment creation for the jobless	
Providing a survival strategy for low-income urban residents	Conflicting urban land issues
Urban agriculture making use of urban wastes	Focus on the urban cultivation activities rather than in relation to broader urban management issues
	Urban agriculture can benefit only the wealthier city dwellers in some cases

Figure 43 Summary of the findings of urban agriculture research

Food produced locally in urban areas may have several added bene-fits. First, it employs a proportion of the city's population. Second, cost – in Addis Ababa dwellers can save between 10% and 20% of their income through urban cultivation. Third, it diversifies the sources of food, resulting in a more secure supply (see Figure 43).

(c) New Cities

For rich countries, there are more options. At one end of the scale are new towns and cities, such as Brasilia, Canberra and Gongju-Yongi in Korea. Gongju-Yongi is a £26 billion scheme to replace Seoul as Korea's capital by 2020 (Figure 44). The relocation is necessary to ease chronic overcrowding in Seoul, for redistribution of the state's wealth and to reduce the danger of a military attack from North Korea. Previous developments have concentrated huge amounts of money, power and up to half of Korea's population in Seoul. Construction begins in 2007. Another impressive scheme is the Malaysian new town of Putrajaya.

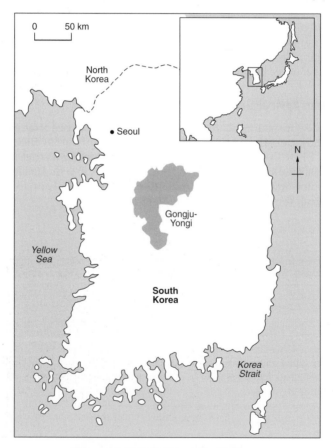

Figure 44 Gongju-Yongi, South Korea

CASE STUDY: PUTRAJAYA NEW TOWN

Putrajaya is a totally new city in Malaysia. Covering an area of 4931 hectares, it is situated 25 km south of the capital city of Kuala Lumpur (Figure 45). Perbadanan Putrajaya was established in 1995.

Putrajaya is a planned city being built according to a series of comprehensive policies and guidelines for land use, transportation system, utilities, infrastructure, housing, public amenities, information technology, parks and gardens.

The **mission** of the Putrajaya Corporation is to:

- provide an efficient and effective administration
- provide quality services to ensure customer satisfaction

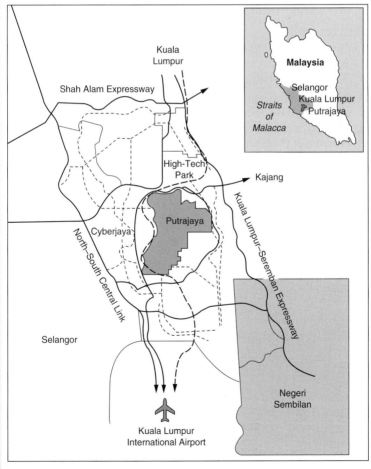

Figure 45 Putrajaya, Malaysia

- provide infrastructure and amenities towards creating an ideal environment for living and working.

Their functions include:

- the functions of a local government in the Perbadanan Putrajaya area
- to promote, stimulate, facilitate, and undertake commercial, infrastructure and residential development in the area
- to promote, stimulate, and undertake economic and social development in the area
- to control and co-ordinate the performance of the above activities in the area.

The master plan and urban design vision of Putrajaya has two main components: the core area and the peripheral area.

The core area

The core area of Putrajaya is divided into four precincts linked by a distinctive 4.2-km long boulevard. The precincts are identified by their predominant economic activities.

- **Precinct 1:** The prime minister's office (Perdana Putra building) and most of the federal government ministries, departments and agencies.
- **Precinct 2:** commercial and government buildings, parks, open spaces (Figure 46) and residential areas.
- **Precinct 3:** ministries and institutions related to the development of the arts and culture.

Figure 46 Wetlands in Putrajaya

Figure 47 New offices in Putrajaya

- **Precinct 4:** the main commercial and business district of Putrajaya convention centre (Figure 47), sport academies and water-based recreational activities.

The peripheral area

Twelve of the precincts make up the residential neighbourhoods. The planning and design of Putrajaya's residential areas is intended to foster a sense of identity through the neighbourhood focal points, landscaping and the treatment of the public realm. A total of 67,000 homes of varying ranges, sizes, types and densities have been planned. Among the facilities provided in the residential areas are schools, hospitals, shopping centres, mosques, multi-purpose halls, learning centres and neighbourhood parks.

Taman wetland, situated in precinct 13 Putrajaya wetland, is the largest constructed freshwater wetland in the tropics. It functions as a flood control system and a natural filter system for the Putrajaya Lake. Apart from providing an expansive area for recreation and education, it forms an essential part of the ecosystem.

Chapter Summary

- Urbanisation is the increase in proportion of people living in urban areas.
- Urbanisation has increased rapidly since 1950.
- The increase has been most rapid in LEDCs.
- One aspect of urbanisation has been the growth of megacities.
- In addition, there are world cities – not necessarily as large as megacities but important players on the world scene.
- World cities have a major role to play in terms of development.
- In many cities, especially in LEDCs, there are major slums.
- Slums have positive as well as negative aspects.
- Slums are found in MEDCs as well as in LEDCs.
- The key to upgrading slums is not housing but employment.
- Most of the problems related to slums result from poverty – increasing income could alleviate many of these problems.
- In MEDCs inequality and deprivation are a manifestation of poverty.
- The housing crisis in LEDCs has many aspects.
- For those with money, new cities and new towns are an attractive way of improving the quality of life within cities.

Questions

1. Suggest how and why deprivation may vary spatially within a large urban area.
2. 'Shanty towns are a solution rather than a problem.' In what ways can shanty towns be considered as solutions? Use examples to support your answer.
3. To what extent is it possible to manage the problems associated with shanty towns?

5 Industry and Trade

1 Globalisation, Industrialisation and Employment

(a) Globalisation

The concept of **globalisation** developed in the 1960s after the Canadian academic Marshall McLuhan used the term **global village** to describe the breakdown of spatial barriers around the world. Globalisation refers to a range of processes and impacts that occur at a global scale, usually economic systems, but it can include physical systems (global warming) and socio-cultural systems (fashion, music, film industry). According to recent commentators such as Legrain (2002) and Waters (2001), globalisation is the way in which people's lives are increasingly intertwined with those of distant people and places, economically, politically and culturally.

McLuhan argued that the similarities between places were greater than the differences between them, and that much of the world had been caught up in the same economic, social and cultural processes. He suggested that economic activities operated at a global scale and that other scales were becoming less important.

There are three main forms of globalisation:

- **economic:** largely caused by the growth of MNCs/TNCs
- **cultural:** the impact of Western culture, art, media, sport and leisure pursuits on the world
- **political:** the growth of Western democracies and their influence on poor countries, and the decline of centralised economies.

While globalisation of economic activity has certainly occurred, and there is evidence of a new international division of labour. The division of labour suggests that, at a crude level of analysis, it is possible to differentiate between two groups.

- The highly skilled, highly paid decision-making, research and managerial occupations. At a national level, these are concentrated in the economic core regions of the country. At a global scale, these occupations are located in MEDCs.
- The unskilled poorly paid assembly occupations. At a national level these 'screwdriver industries' are located in the cheap peripheral parts. Assembly production is located in LEDCs that offer low labour costs.

(b) Industrialisation and Employment

The so-called new international division of labour (NIDL) is central to globalisation, creating changes in production by world region. The NIDL refers to the spatial arrangement of labour – highly skilled research and development, and decision-making jobs are located in the core (MEDCs) while low-cost production occurs in LEDCs and peripheral areas of MEDCs. At least three NIDLs can be recognised:

- at the time of European colonisation
- the industrial development of certain semi-developed areas at the end of the nineteenth century
- the present era, in which foreign direct investment (FDI) has expanded greatly.

Recent trends have seen widespread deregulation and liberalisation, after an earlier era that emphasised protectionism.

(c) Global Shift: Industrialisation and Development

The past 30 years have seen a global shift in the NIDL, in which some LEDCs have become newly industrialising countries (NICs). The traditional division of labour in which MEDCs countries produced the industrial goods and the LEDCs produced the primary goods was always an oversimplification. Now it is simply wrong. By the late 1990s almost 50% of manufacturing jobs were located in the LEDCs and over 60% of LEDC exports to MEDCs were of manufactured goods, a 1200% increase since 1960.

One explanation for these changes can be found in the growing globalisation of production. Transnational companies (TNCs), which operate in at least one country beyond that of their origin, are major agents in this globalisation process. They may invest overseas to take advantage of market access, cheap labour, lack of regulation (such as rules concerning the environment), tax breaks, or access to raw materials. Critics argue that TNCs are agents of exploitation. For example, the use of cheap labour amounts to exploitation, and intra-firm trade and capital mobility allows these companies to evade tax payments.

The continued concentration of industrial production in selected areas is reflected in the figures on foreign investment. Most direct foreign investment is located in the MEDCs, and the late 1990s saw a fall in the proportion going to LEDCs. This was largely because of the recession in east Asia, which itself shows how concentrated foreign investment is in the developing world.

The global economy therefore continues to be characterised by polarisation, with some people and regions at the cutting edge of globalisation while others are marginalised. TNCs tend to be highly selective in their choice of investment location, concentrating in parts of MEDCs, although China and Vietnam are major beneficiaries of FDI.

(d) The New International Division of Labour

Most areas of the world now constitute part of the global market. The production of clothes, shoes, bicycles and televisions has become global (Figure 48). The NIDL has recently been characterised by the globalisation of services and particularly producer services.

To some, the most important feature of NIDLs is the change it has brought in the role of the state. Power has shifted from the nation-state to the transnational corporation. For example, the world's 37,000 parent transnational corporations control 75% of all world

Figure 48 Liverpool football – made in India

trade in commodities, manufactured goods and services. One-third of this trade is intra-firm – making it very difficult for governments and international trade organisations to exert any control.

CASE STUDY: CHINA'S ECONOMY

China's successful bid to industrialise has resulted in them having a trade surplus with the USA and attracting $57 billion of foreign investment in 2003, particularly by metal industries. However, the infrastructure is now under strain, the power grid in particular and some workers are still unhappy. High levels of unemployment in rural areas are worsened by the inability for them to move out due to prohibitive costs in urban areas. The government is trying to address this through cutting taxes for farmers and improving medical and education facilities in rural areas. The government is also trying to curb spending by reducing the amount of lending by banks.

(e) Comparing China and India – Impressive Growth, Important Differences

China and India, together containing a third of the world's population, have experienced tremendous economic growth since 1990. Their successes in advancing average well-being imply major improvements for a large portion of humanity. Although both countries have achieved rapid, sustained economic growth, their rates of progress have been quite different. China has enjoyed the fastest sustained economic advance in human history, averaging real per capita growth of 8% a year over the past decade. Its per capita income is now $3976 in PPP terms. Meanwhile, real per capita income in India grew at an average rate of 4.4%, reaching $2358 in 2001. Reflecting their successful economic growth, both countries have seen significant reductions in poverty. The World Bank estimates that the proportion of people living on less than $1 a day declined in China from 33% in 1990 to 16% in 2000 and in India from 42% in 1993–1994 to 35% in 2001.

China's exceptional growth is partly explained by its market-based reforms that started in 1978, well before India's reforms in 1991. These reforms have enabled China to integrate with the global economy at a phenomenal pace. Today it is the largest recipient of foreign direct investment among LEDCs, with annual investment rising from almost zero in 1978 to about $52 billion in 2002 (nearly 5% of GDP). FDI in India has also increased significantly, although at much lower levels, growing from $129 million in 1991 to $4 billion in 2002 (less than 1% of GDP).

Strong export growth has contributed to the economic performance of both countries, with a growing dominance of manufactured exports – although again China has had much more success in this area. Its exports reached $320 billion in 2001, compared with $35 billion for India. Manufactured exports accounted for 53% of China's total exports in 1981 and for 90% in 2001; in India that share rose from 60% to 77%. China has had particular success in moving from labour-intensive to technology-intensive exports: telecommunications equipment and computers now account for a quarter of its exports.

Social investments are required for sustained economic growth. In China public spending on education is 2.3% of GDP while that on health is 2.1% of GDP. Literacy stands at 84%, infant mortality rates at 32 per 1000 live births and under-5 mortality rates at 40 per 1000 live births. India, in contrast, has traditionally had lower spending levels. Health spending stands at 1.3% of GDP (central and state governments combined). Spending on education has increased significantly, from 0.8% of GDP in 1950 to 3.2% today, although it still falls short of the government target of 6% of GDP. Human development indicators for India remain much lower than for China. Literacy stands at 65%, infant mortality at 68 per 1000 live births and under-5 mortality rates at 96 per 1000 live births.

It would be misleading to talk solely in terms of national averages for two countries so large in population and area. In China the highest economic growth has occurred in the coastal provinces – while the geographically isolated north-western provinces have experienced much lower growth. India also harbours stark regional variations. From 1992 to 1997 per capita economic growth ranged from −0.2% in Bihar to 7.8% in Gujarat.

Both India and China face the challenge of fostering a knowledge-based economy to maintain consistently high economic growth as average skill levels increase. Both also need to focus on spreading the gains of growth to regions, communities and ethnic groups that have seen so little benefit from the new prosperity.

CASE STUDY: VIETNAM

Vietnam has the second best-performing economy in Asia at the moment (see Figure 49)and has grown by around 7.4% for the past 10 years. The growth has meant that the number of people considered to be living in poverty in 1993 has approximately halved (from 58% to 29%), according to the World Bank.

There have been a number of reasons for the growth of the economy. Agricultural reform which saw land being passed from the state to the rural poor began the economic growth process, but more recently a growth in exports and foreign direct investments have been the cause of the increase.

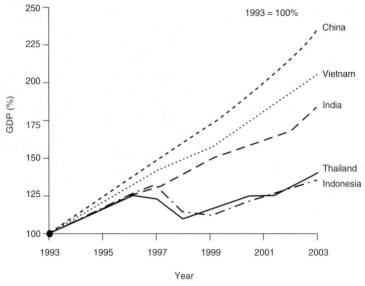

Figure 49 Growth in Vietnam

Exports, especially to the USA, increased between 2001 and 2003; for example, the textile export to the USA grew from $47 million to $2.4 billion in that time. Exports were up generally by 20%. Vietnam not only trades with the USA though, it is a trading partner with countries in Europe, south-east Asia, including China, and Australia.

Small industries are also booming, with 50,000 opening up in 2002. However, it is again the rural areas that are faring the worst where the government's economic reform has least impact.

2 The Informal Sector

(a) The Informal Sector and Employment

The 'informal sector' is often equated with precarious, low-productivity, poorly remunerated employment in Third World cities, although in reality the sector is highly heterogeneous. Moreover, although many people in the informal sector work on their own account in street vending, the running of 'frontroom' eateries, stalls or shops (Figure 50).

Government officials, planners and social scientists have come round to the notion that the informal sector is more of a seedbed of economic potential than a 'poverty trap'. Some informal workers earn more than salaried workers; self-employment can be a source of pride or prestige, informality permits flexibility and ready adaptation to

Formal sector	Informal sector
Large scale	Small scale
Modern	Traditional
Corporate ownership	Family/individual ownership
Capital-intensive	Labour-intensive
Profit-oriented	Subsistence-oriented
Imported technology/inputs	Indigenous technology/inputs
Protected market (e.g. tariffs, quotas)	Unregulated/competitive markets
Difficult entry	Ease of entry
Formally acquired skills (e.g. school/ college education)	Informally acquired skills (e.g. in home or craft apprenticeship)
Majority of workers protected by labour legislation and covered by social security	Minority of workers protected by labour legislation and covered by social security

Figure 50 Common characteristics used to define formal and informal employment

changing demand and family circumstances, and people often acquire skills in the formal sector that can subsequently be used to advantage in their own businesses.

Regardless of policies that may be implemented by governments and agencies, it is likely that the informal sector will continue to be a significant feature of LEDC urban labour markets in the twenty-first century. Accepting this, measures are arguably needed to help it operate more efficiently and with better conditions for its workers.

(b) Child Labour

Child labour takes on many forms, from paid work in factories and other forms of waged labour such as street selling, which is particularly characteristic in cities, to unwaged labour in the household and predominantly rural areas, to bonded labour and trafficked labour, which are both forms of slavery. Industries, often export-oriented, that employ children have received the most attention and include the production of carpets, glassware, matches, fireworks, gem polishing and quarrying.

Of the estimated 250 million working children aged between 5 and 15 years in developing countries, the International Labour Organization (ILO) estimated that 61% are located in Asia, 32% in Africa and 7% in Latin America. The ILO estimates that less than 5% of child labourers are employed in export manufacturing, while 90% of working children in rural households across the developing world are believed to be engaged in some form of agricultural activity (see Figure 51).

Children have the right to:

- enough food, clean water and health care
- an adequate standard of living
- be with their family or those who will care for them best
- protection from all exploitation, physical, mental and sexual abuse
- special protection when exposed to armed conflict
- be protected from all forms of discrimination
- be protected from work that threatens their education, health or development
- special care and training if disabled
- play
- education
- have their own opinions taken into account in decisions which affect their lives
- know what their rights are

Figure 51 The United Nations Convention on the Rights of the Child, 1989

3 Export Processing Zones and Free Trade

Export processing zones (EPZs) and free-trade zones (FTZs) are important parts of the so-called new international division of labour, and represent what are seen as relatively easy paths to industrialisation. By the end of the twentieth century, over 90 countries had established EPZs as part of their economic strategies.

Export processing zones (EPZs) have been defined as labour-intensive manufacturing centres that involve the import of raw materials and the export of factory products. **Free-trade zones** can be classified as zones in which manufacturing does not have to take place in order to gain trading privileges and, hence, such zones have become more characterised by retailing.

The popularity of EPZs in the latter decades of the twentieth century can be attributed to three groups of factors that link the economies of LEDCs with those of the world economy in general and the advanced economies in particular:

- problems of indebtedness and serious foreign exchange shortfalls in LEDCs since the 1980s
- the spread of new-liberal ideas in the 1990s that encouraged open economies, foreign investment and non-traditional exports
- the search by multinational corporations (MNCs) for cost-saving locations, particularly in terms of wage costs, in order to shift manufacturing, assembly and component production from locations in the advanced economies.

The feasibility of MNCs relocating manufacturing capacity to EPZs was also improved by the possibility of decentralising standardised production processes. As the assembly of products became more standardised it proved profitable for MNCs to shift standardised production to low labour cost locations.

In EPZ locations there was normally an added bonus for the MNC, as LEDC governments offered them more favourable investment, trade, tax and labour conditions. Concessions included:

- trade: the elimination of customs duties on imports
- investment: liberalisation of capital flows and occasionally access to special financial credits
- important investments in the provision of local infrastructure by central and/or local government of the host country
- taxation: reduction or exemption from federal, state and local taxes
- labour relations: limitations on labour legislation that apply in the rest of the country, such as the presence of trade unions and the adherence to minimum wage and working hours legislation.

Within LEDCs, EPZs have been established in a wide range of environments – from border areas (as in north Mexico) and relatively undeveloped regions, to locations adjacent to large cities. The most common location has been on the coast, as in the case of China. EPZs have been most concentrated in the Asia-Pacific region, where in the 1990s approximately 40% of EPZs were located but where two-thirds of employment in EPZs was generated. Latin America and the Caribbean is the next most significant region for EPZs.

The creation of EPZs has been a popular policy for governments of LEDCs because they represent a relatively easy path to begin industrialisation in a country. The MNCs normally provides technology, capital, inputs and the export markets.

Although the establishment of an EPZ could be seen as beneficial in the short term for the LEDC, in the long term it offers a major problem as regards economic sustainability. MNCs are normally attracted by trade and tax incentives, low labour costs and labour flexibility to locate a branch plant in an EPZ. Thus, a reliance on simple export processing would at best perpetuate a reliance on low-skilled, labour-intensive assembly and at worst would see the premature end of this type of manufacturing activity within the developing country.

Mexico's 'classic' export processing zone was characterised by low-skilled, labour-intensive assembly plants specialising in clothing, footwear and basic electronics. The primary economic agents were the MNCs that supplied technology, capital, material inputs and export market. The production of components was largely organised through subsidiaries of MNCs (such as Ford) rather than by national/local firms producing for MNCs through sub-contracts (more the case in east Asian EPZs).

In east Asia, there have been other versions of EPZs. In certain countries, such as South Korea and Taiwan, EPZs were an important part of the early rapid phase of industrial growth. In these countries, governments were active and successful in promoting EPZs, although their initiatives were associated with a wide range of other inward investment and export promotion incentives. The key factors in such a comparison are the importance of national firms in export-oriented manufacturing, the technological capability acquired by those firms and the role of government in effectively promoting export-oriented industrialisation.

4 Small Island Economies

Small island economies (SIEs) are a type of economy with particular characteristics and problems. Small generally refers to a population of less than one million. Being an island suggests relative isolation and remoteness, and an impoverished access to the markets compared with larger countries that share land-based national boundaries with neighbouring states. (Equally countries without access to the coast may be considered to have reduced access to trade and may be dependent on the good will of their neighbours.) SIEs are independent, so this excludes dependencies such as Montserrat, Martinique, Tahiti and the US Virgin Islands, even though they may display many of the characteristics of small island economies.

There are a number of different small island economies, in different parts of the world such as:

- the Pacific excluding Papua New Guinea
- the Caribbean excluding Jamaica and Trinidad
- others such as Maldives, Seychelles, Cape Verde, East Timor.

The Pacific/Caribbean comparison is a good one. For example, the Caribbean SIEs have considerably longer experience of trying to attract FDI and are more favourably positioned to attract North American FDI, as well as to make inroads into the North American market (e.g. North American tourist services).

(a) SIEs in the Caribbean

Some of the Caribbean SIEs face big debt problems (over 100% of GDP in Dominica and Antigua), the result of economic mismanagement, declining tourism revenues and changing trade rules.

The Caribbean has the world's largest group of SIEs (Figure 52). The islands argue that their small size makes it harder to cope with trouble. Preferential trade arrangements for Caribbean producers of bananas go in 2006, and for sugar by 2009. The loss of these industries hits deep. Dominica exported $24 million of bananas in 1993 but only $9 million in 2000. Without protection, only Guyana and Belize can compete with Brazil in sugar production – and then only with modernisation and job losses.

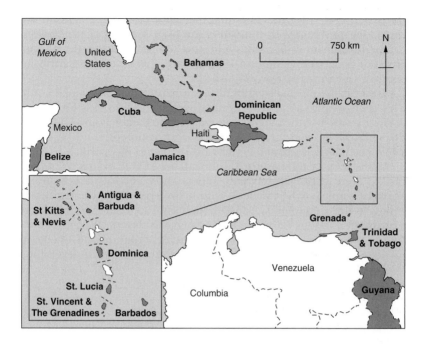

Country	GDP ($, billions)	Tourism earnings (% of GDP)	Cannabis seizures (tonnes)
Antigua & Barbuda	0.7	44	0.1
Bahamas	4.8	38	0
Barbados	2.3	27	2.6
Belize	0.7	17	0.2
Cuba	24	8	5.5
Dominica	0.3	18	0.5
Dominican Republic	19.6	15	1.5
Grenada	0.4	17	0.1
Guyana	0.1	58	0.1
Jamaica	7.7	17	55.9
St Kitts & Nevis	0.3	18	0.1
St Lucia	0.7	39	1.8
St Vincent & The Grenadines	0.3	22	1.7
Trinidad & Tobago	7.7	3	3.3

Figure 52 Caribbean SIEs

The main earner for most Caribbean SIEs is tourism. It has fluctuated ever since the 11 September 2001 terrorist attacks on the USA. One problem with tourism is the high running cost of hotels, competition from cruise ships and new resorts. Tourism needs stability, but drug trafficking and violence are giving certain Caribbean countries a bad reputation (Figure 52).

However, being small is not always a handicap. Some small countries, such as Singapore, are very wealthy. The most thriving Caribbean economies are not the biggest, but include the Bahamas and Barbados, through tourism and financial services. One competitive advantage of a small economy is the ability to be hospitable to the world.

The islands of the eastern Caribbean are rich in resources, which can be used to provide services. Where those services can be transported cheaply (such as via a telephone link), or where the consumer comes to the area to collect them (such as in tourism), the transport cost disadvantage is minimised. This suggests that most of the countries in the region will need to exploit their comparative advantage in services, including but not limited to tourism, as a way of developing their income potential.

CASE STUDY: ST LUCIA

St Lucia's economy is relatively stable, if not very strong. Tourism has replaced agriculture as the most important part of the economy. It now accounts for 12% of GDP and a third of St Lucia's working population are employed in tourism and tourism-related jobs. Tourism is seen as the way forward in St Lucia, and there have been many recent developments and extensions to St Lucia's tourism base, such as the expansion of the Rodney Bay resort, near Gros Islet north of the capital, Castries.

Agriculture is the second most important industry, involving about one-third of the working population. The most important crop being bananas that earn about 40% of St Lucia's export earnings. Most of the farms are small family farms and the bananas are marketed through the St Lucia Banana Corporation.

In recent years banana wars have had a devastating impact on St Lucia's economy. St Lucia's bananas are not very competitive compared with the US firms based in Central America. However, they have benefited from a special trading arrangement with the European Union; the World Trade Organization has declared this arrangement illegal. Although St Lucia farmers have tried to diversify (broaden) their agriculture there has been limited success.

The International Monetary Fund (IMF) has welcomed the recent strengthening of the St Lucian economy and the reduction in unemployment, stemming from the stabilisation of banana production and the development of tourism along with related activities.

After a period of slow growth in the mid-1990s, mainly due to a decline in banana output, economic growth has improved since 1998.

The manufacturing sector in St Lucia comprises just over 170 firms, of which more than half (55%) employ fewer than 10 workers. In 1999 manufactured exports amounted to less than 5% of St Lucia's export of goods and services. St Lucia has severe shortages of appropriate technical skills, resulting in low productivity. The most common areas of manufacturing include textiles, handicrafts and furniture.

Thus, for good or bad, St Lucia's economic success is closely connected with the success or otherwise of the tourism sector. In the light of the 11 September 2001 terrorist attacks on the USA, and the likelihood of global recession, tourism might not be the cure that once it had seemed.

5 Debt and Development

There are many ways in which underdevelopment may be addressed. Unfair trading patterns are one of the causes of the development gap. MEDCs account for 75% of the world's exports and over 80% of manufactured exports. The pattern is complicated by flows of FDI, and the internal trade within TNCs. Most of the flow of profits is back to MEDCs, while an increasing share of FDI is to NICs. Reform of trade is necessary to protect LEDCs and small countries.

The main regulatory bodies include:

- international regulators such as the International Monetary Fund (IMF) and the World Trade Organization (WTO)
- co-ordinating groups of countries such as the G8
- regional trading blocs such as the European Union (EU), North American Free Trade Association (NAFTA) and Association of South East Asian Nations (ASEAN)
- national governments.

However, much of the trade and money exchange that takes place is run by stock exchanges and the world's main banks. For example, Barclays Capital is the investment-banking sector of Barclays Bank. It deals with over £360 billion of investment through its 33 offices located throughout the world. Its regional headquarters are located mostly in MEDCs such as London, Paris, Frankfurt, New York and Tokyo. Hong Kong is the exception, although it is an important financial centre, like most of the other cities on the list.

There is widespread criticism that many of the regulatory bodies have limited power, and that when faced with a powerful MEDC or TNC they capitulate.

(a) Poor Countries' Debt

Sub-Saharan Africa includes most of the 42 countries classified as heavily indebted and 25 of the 32 countries rated as severely indebted. In 1962, sub-Saharan Africa owed $3 billion. Twenty years later it had reached $142 billion. Today it's about $235 billion. The most heavily indebted countries are Nigeria ($35 billion), Côte d'Ivoire ($19 billion) and Sudan ($18 billion).

Many developing countries borrowed heavily in the 1970s and early 1980s, encouraged to do so by Western lenders, including export credit agencies. They soon ran into problems:

- low growth in industrialised economies
- high interest rates between 1975 and 1985
- rise in oil prices
- falling commodity prices.

(b) The Heavily Indebted Poor Countries Initiative

The Heavily Indebted Poor Countries (HIPCs) initiative, launched in 1996 by the IMF and the World Bank and endorsed by 180 governments, has two main objectives:

- to relieve certain low-income countries of their unsustainable debt to donors
- to promote reform and sound policies for growth, human development and poverty reduction.

Debt relief occurs in two steps:

- at the decision point the country gets debt **service relief** after having demonstrated adherence to an IMF programme and progress in developing a national poverty strategy
- at the completion point the country gets debt **stock relief** on approval by the World Bank and the IMF of its Poverty Reduction Strategy Paper. The country is entitled to at least 90% debt relief from bilateral and multilateral creditors to make debt levels sustainable.

Of the 42 countries participating in the initiative, 34 are in sub-Saharan Africa. None had a PPP above $1500 in 2001, and all rank low on the HDI. Between 1990 and 2001 HIPCs grew by an average of just 0.5% a year.

HIPCs have been overindebted for at least 20 years: by poor country standards their ratios of debt to exports were already high in the 1980s. At the same time, HIPCs have received considerable official development assistance. Net transfers of such aid averaged about 10%

of their GNP in the 1990s, compared with about 2% for all poor countries. To date 16 HIPCs have reached the decision point and eight have reached the completion point (Benin, Bolivia, Burkina Faso, Mali, Mauritania, Mozambique, Tanzania, Uganda).

Expanding market access is essential to help countries diversify and expand trade. Trade policies in rich countries remain highly discriminatory against developing country exports. Average OECD tariffs on manufactured goods from developing countries are more than four times those on manufactured goods from other OECD countries. Moreover, agricultural subsidies in rich countries lead to unfair competition. Cotton farmers in Benin, Burkina Faso, Chad, Mali and Togo have improved productivity and achieved lower production costs than their richer country competitors. Still, they can barely compete. Rich country agricultural subsidies total more than $300 billion a year – nearly six times official development assistance.

Since 1988, the 'Paris Club' of government creditors has approved a series of debt relief initiatives. In addition, the World Bank has lent more through its concessional lending arm and the International Development Agency has given loans for up to 50 years without interest but with a 0.75% service charge. Lending has risen from $424 million in 1980 to $2.9 billion plus a further $928 million through the African Development Bank. The IMF has also introduced a **soft loan facility** conditional on wide-ranging economic reforms.

In addition, MEDCs should set targets to:

- Increase official development assistance to fill financing gaps (estimated to be at least $50 billion).
- Remove tariffs and quotas on agricultural products, textiles and clothing exported by developing countries.
- Remove subsidies on agricultural exports from developing countries.
- Agree and finance, for HIPCs, a compensatory financing facility for external shocks – including collapses in commodity prices.
- Agree and finance deeper debt reduction for HIPCs having reached their completion points to ensure sustainability.

(c) Structural Adjustment Programmes (SAPs)

Structural adjustment programmes (SAPs) were designed to cut government expenditure, reduce the amount of state intervention in the economy, and promote liberalisation and international trade. SAPs were explicit about the need for international trade.

SAPs consist of four main elements:

- greater use of a country's resource base
- policy reforms to increase economic efficiency
- generation of foreign income through diversification of the economy and increased trade
- reducing the active role of the state.

These were sometimes divided into two main groups: the **stabilisation measures** – short-term steps to limit any further deterioration of the economy (e.g. wage freeze, reduced subsidies on food, health and education); and **adjustment measures** – longer term policies to boost economic competitiveness (tax reductions, export promotion, downsizing of the civil service, privatisation and economic liberalisation).

6 Trading Blocs

A trading bloc is an arrangement among a group of nations to allow free trade between member countries but to impose tariffs (charges) on other countries who may wish to trade with them. The European Union (EU) is an excellent example of a trading bloc. Many trading blocs were established after the Second World War as countries used political ties to further their economic development. There are a number of regionally based trading blocs (Figure 53).

Within a trading bloc, member countries have free access to each other's markets. Thus, in the EU, the UK has access to Spanish markets, German markets and so on. However, Spain, Germany and the other countries of the EU have access to Britain's market. Being a member of a trading bloc is important as it allows greater market access – in the case of the EU this amounts to over 470 million wealthy consumers.

Some critics believe that trading blocs are unfair as they deny access to non-members. So, for example, countries from the developing

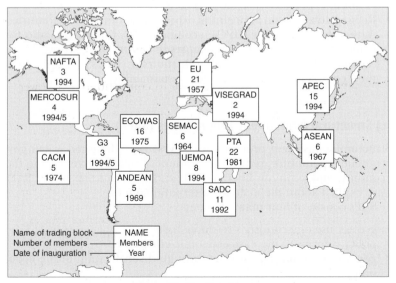

Figure 53 Trading blocs

world have more limited access to the rich markets of Europe. This makes it harder for them to trade, and to develop. In order to limit the amount of protectionism the WTO has tried to promote free trade. This would allow equal access to all producers to all markets.

CASE STUDY: NAFTA

The North American Free Trade Agreement (NAFTA) between the USA, Canada and Mexico was signed in 1994, creating one of the largest free trade zones in the world. It is the first to join countries from MEDCs and LEDCs. It is an agreement to phase out restrictions on the movement of goods, services and capital between the three countries by the year 2010. Its aim is to:

- eliminate trade barriers
- promote economic competition
- increase investment opportunities
- improve co-operation between the USA, Canada and Mexico.

Until 1982 Mexico followed a policy of government-sponsored industrialisation based on import substitution industries (ISIs). However, financial crises through overspending, in the 1970s and 1980s forced the Mexican government to seek aid from the USA, the World Bank and the IMF. Aid was provided, at a price: Mexico was forced to rearrange its economy along free market lines.

The government was keen to agree, partly to receive the aid and partly in fear of being ignored by the USA. Mexico hoped that by joining NAFTA economic growth would follow, employment increase and it would take off as an NIC.

However, there has been opposition to NAFTA. Critics argue that it will not necessarily bring economic growth. Experience in Canada has shown that:

- many small firms have closed due to competition with lower cost US firms
- many firms left Canada for lower cost areas in the USA
- mergers and takeovers have led to increased unemployment.

With respect to Mexico:

- US industries will move to Mexico to take advantage of its ultra-cheap labour, thereby creating unemployment in the USA and reinforcing a low-wage mentality in Mexico
- up to 15 million farmers will be affected by the removal of subsidies, decline in communal ownership of the land and the removal of border restrictions on trade. US and Canadian grain producers will dump their surpluses in Mexico, forcing uncompetitive Mexican peasants out of agriculture.

According to NAFTA, Mexico's rural areas will become export-orientated: industrial and service growth will replace agriculture. However, where there has already been growth its value has been questioned. Along the US–Mexican border there are about 2000 US-owned, labour-intensive, export-orientated assembly plants, employing about 500,000 Mexican labourers. Many of the workers are children, wages are low and working conditions unsafe. Critics argue that Mexico could be exploited even more as a huge ultra-cheap labour supply.

Environmentalists point to Mexico's poor record of enforcing environmental laws. They fear that Mexico may become a dumping ground for hazardous material and show that Mexico's rivers and air are already heavily polluted.

7 Fair Trade or Ethical Trade

Fair or ethical trade can be defined as trade that attempts to be socially, economically and environmentally responsible. It is trade in which companies take responsibility for the wider impact of their business. Ethical trading is an attempt to address failings of the global trading system.

Good examples of fair trading include Prudent Exports and Blue Skies, both pineapple-exporting companies in Ghana. Prudent Exports, which grows as well as exports pineapples, has introduced better working conditions for its farmers, including longer contracts and better wages. Prudent Exports has its own farms, buys pineapples from small holders and exports directly to European supermarkets. They have also responded to requests to cut back on the use of pesticides and chemical fertilisers. The result has been an increase in productivity and sales, supplying a leading British supermarket. Indeed, some retailers appear to be the driving force behind fair trade as they seek out good practice in their suppliers in terms of health and safety at work, employment of children, pay and conditions, and even the freedom of association of workers.

Nevertheless, there are conflicts of interest. For many Western consumers, fair trade means banning pesticides or banning the use of child labour. Yet in many LEDCs it is normal for children to help out on farms, just as it was in the UK in the late nineteenth and early twentieth centuries. Most LEDC farmers would prefer to send their children to school, but if the price they receive for their produce is low than they cannot afford the school fees. If Western consumers want to stop child labour on farms, they may have to pay high prices for the food they buy.

Chapter Summary

- Globalisation refers to the breakdown of spatial barriers and the integration of the world economy, as well as integration of political and cultural systems.
- Manufacturing industry illustrates a new international division of labour of which highly skilled research and development, and decision-making jobs are located in the core (MEDCs) while low-cost production occurs in LEDCs and peripheral areas of MEDCs.
- This is partly the result of TNCs, companies that have commercial interests in more than one country.
- Globalisation has seen the growth of a number of economies such as China and Vietnam, both of which altered political systems to fuel economic growth.
- There are interesting differences in economic growth in China and India, the world's two most populous countries.
- The informal sector is a major source of income in some LEDCs.
- In some countries, child labour is heavily exploited.
- Many countries have attempted to industrialise using EPZs.
- SIEs face a number of problems. They have, nevertheless, certain advantages such as culture and insularity.
- Certain countries are among the world's poorest – they make up the HIPC.
- To succeed economically HIPCs need access to the world's markets.
- Trading blocs such as the EU and NAFTA limit access of LEDC producers to their markets.
- Fair or ethical trade is trade that attempts to be socially, economically and environmentally responsible.

Questions

1. Who are likely to be the main (a) winners and (b) losers as a result of trading blocs such as NAFTA. Explain your answer.
2. Outline the main issues in developing small island economies.
3. To what extent is it possible to reduce debt among the HIPCs?
4. Explain what is meant by the term 'new international division of labour' (NIDL). Examine the relationship between the NIDL and globalisation.

6 Environment and Development

KEY TERMS

Environmental determinism A belief that the environment to a large extent controls human response.
Biometeorology The study of how weather and climate affects people.
Deforestation The partial or complete removal of areas of forests for timber or for other land uses.
Global warming The recent increase of world temperatures largely as a result of increases in greenhouse gases.
Biodiversity Genetic variety – some ecosystems such as rainforests and coral reefs are very rich in biodiversity but are disappearing fast.

1 Introduction

The physical environment has a major impact on levels of development. Some environments offer many opportunities for development, e.g. fertile soils, a plentiful supply of water and numerous resources, while others limit development through a lack of water, infertile soils and a lack of resources. Other environments experience repeated hazards, which limit the economic and social development of the country. Many LEDCs such as Bangladesh, Mozambique and parts of Brazil are underdeveloped on account of their physical environment.

There is an uneven geography of resource allocation, resource consumption, environmental damage and human impact. Rich countries generate most of the world's environmental pollution and deplete many of its natural resources. Key examples include depletion of the world's forests and emissions of greenhouse gases that cause climate change, both of which are tied to unsustainable consumption patterns by rich people and countries. There are many ways in which the environment has major effects on development issues (Figure 54). These include direct effects on food production and health, and indirect effects on education, poverty, access to health care and gender empowerment.

2 Climate and Development

There are many links between climate and development (Figure 55). **Biometeorology** is the study of how weather and climate affects food supply, health and levels of comfort. **Environmental determinism**

Millennium Development Goal	Links to the environment
Eradicate extreme poverty and hunger	Poor people's livelihoods and food security often depend on ecosystem goods and services. Poor people tend to have insecure rights to environmental resources and inadequate access to markets, decision making and environmental information – limiting their capability to protect the environment and improve their livelihoods and well-being. Lack of access to energy services also limits productive opportunities, especially in rural areas
Achieve universal primary education	Time spent collecting water and fuel wood reduces time available for schooling. In addition, the lack of energy, water and sanitation services in rural areas discourages qualified teachers from working in poor villages
Promote gender equality and empower women	Women and girls are especially burdened by water and fuel collection, reducing their time and opportunities for education, literacy and income-generating activities. Women often have unequal rights and insecure access to land and other natural resources, limiting their opportunities and ability to access other productive assets
Reduce child mortality	Diseases (such as diarrhoea) tied to unclean water and inadequate sanitation and respiratory infections related to pollution are among the leading killers of children under 5. Lack of fuel for boiling water also contributes to preventable water-borne diseases
Improve maternal health	Inhaling polluted indoor air and carrying heavy loads of water and fuel wood damages women's health and can make them less fit to bear children, with greater risks of complications during pregnancy. Lack of energy for illumination and refrigeration, as well as inadequate sanitation, undermine health care, especially in rural areas
Combat major diseases	Up to 20% of the disease burden in developing countries may be due to environmental risk factors (as with malaria and parasitic infections). Preventive measures to reduce such hazards are as important as treatment – and often more cost-effective. New biodiversity-derived medicines hold promise for fighting major diseases

Figure 54 Links between the environment and Millennium Development Goals

states that the environment to a large extent controls human response, whereas **environmental possibilism** suggests that people may operate differently within environmental parameters (see *Climate and Society* in this series). Extreme events can have a huge impact on human lives – the Bangladesh floods of 2004 are a good example. However, even the normal range of weather influences human activities (Figure 55).

Primary sector	General activities	Specific activities
Food	Agriculture Fisheries	Land use, crop scheduling and operations, hazard control, productivity, livestock and irrigation, pests and diseases Management, operations, yield
Water	Water disasters Water resources	Flood-, drought-, pollution-abatement Engineering design, supply operations
Health and community	Human biometeorology Human comfort Air pollution Tourism and recreation	Health, disease, morbidity and mortality Settlement design, heating and ventilation, clothing, acclimatisation Potential, dispersion, control Sites, facilities, equipment marketing, sports activities
Energy	Fossil fuels Renewable resources	Distribution, utilisation, conservation Solar-, wind-, water-power development
Industry and trade	Building and construction Communications Forestry Transportation Commerce Services	Sites, design, performance operations, safety Engineering design, construction Regeneration, productivity, biological hazards, fire Air, water and land facilities, scheduling, operations, safety Plant operations, product design, storage of materials, sales planning, absenteeism, accidents Finance, law, insurance, sales

Figure 55 The challenges of weather and climate for economic activities. *Source*: Goudie (1994)

(a) How Global Climate Change Threatens LEDCs

Global climate change is expected to increase the inequalities between MEDCs and LEDCs. The estimated damage for LEDCs partly reflects their weaker adaptive capacity. Hence, climate change is a major development issue. In MEDCs per capita carbon dioxide emissions are 12.4 tonnes – while in LEDCs it is 1.0 tonne.

Climate change could lead to large-scale, possibly irreversible changes in the Earth's systems, with effects at the global and continental levels:

- Reduced crop yields in most tropical and sub-tropical regions and increased variability in agricultural productivity due to extreme weather conditions (droughts and floods).
- Increased variability of precipitation during Asian summer monsoons, which could reduce food production and increase hunger.
- Reduced water availability in many water-scarce regions, particularly sub-tropical regions. Increased water availability in some water-scarce regions – such as parts of south-east Asia.
- Increased destruction of coral reefs and coastal ecosystems and changes in ocean-supported weather patterns.
- With a 1-metre rise in sea level, partly due to global warming, Egypt could see 12% of its territory – home to seven million people – disappear. Rising seas threaten to make several small island nations – such as the Maldives and Tuvalu – uninhabitable, and to swamp vast areas of other countries.
- Increased exposure to vector-borne diseases (malaria, dengue fever) and water-borne diseases (cholera).

(b) Policy Responses to Climate Change

Scientific evidence strongly supports immediate action to curb the greenhouse gas emissions linked with global warming. The 1997 Kyoto Protocol places most of this burden on MEDCs – they contain 16% of the world's population, but generate 51% of such emissions.

The Protocol calls on MEDCs to reduce carbon dioxide emissions by at least 5% of 1990 levels by 2008. Supporters of the Protocol see this as an important step towards managing climate change. Opponents are against it on account of cost, and for a lack of emission limits for poor countries. Another criticism is that, even if fully implemented, the protocol would reduce the average global temperature by less than 0.15°C by 2100.

The USA, which produces 25% of global greenhouse gas emissions, has refused to ratify the Kyoto Protocol. Without US participation, no international agreement on climate change is likely to significantly reduce the threat of global warming. But international co-operation is required to provide incentives for the private sector, consumers and governments to reduce greenhouse gas emissions.

To increase acceptance of the Protocol, more attention should be paid to minimising the costs of combating climate change. It will also be important to build on the Clean Development Mechanism, which permits reductions in carbon emissions through innovative international trading systems. In addition, there is scope for long-term reductions in greenhouse gas emissions beyond the terms of the Kyoto Protocol:

- Developing clean energy technologies – solar or wind energy, fuel cells, hydropower, geothermal energy – that release little or no carbon dioxide. Making these technologies cost-competitive with fossil fuels will require increasing public investment in research and development and removing fossil-fuel subsidies.
- Developing safe, economical technologies that prevent the release of carbon dioxide into the atmosphere. Promising examples include natural carbon sinks such as forests, deep seas and mines, and chemical fixation of carbon dioxide as thermodynamically stable metal carbonates.
- Increasing energy efficiency through more efficient vehicles, appliances, lighting and industrial motors, and through reduced electricity transmission losses.

(c) Arid Environments and Their Management

Arid conditions are caused by a number of factors (see Figure 56).

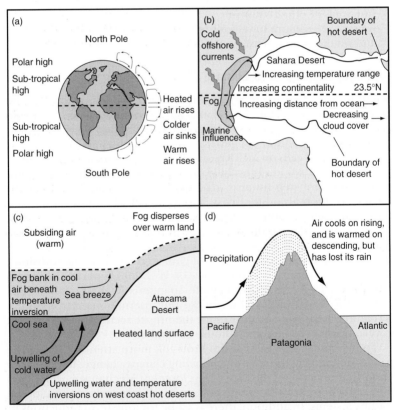

Figure 56 Causes of aridity. (a) Sub-tropical high-pressure, (b) continentality, (c) cold off-shore currents and (d) rain shadow effect

- The main cause is the global atmospheric circulation. Dry, descending air associated with the **sub-tropical anticylones** is the main cause of aridity around 20°–30° north and south.
- Distance from sea, **continentality**, limits the amount of water carried across by winds.
- In other areas, such as the Atacama and Namib deserts, **cold offshore currents** (the Agulhas and Peruvian currents, respectively) limit the amount of water vapour in the overlying air.
- Others are caused by intense **rain shadow effects**, as air passes over mountains. This is certainly true of the Patagonian desert on the leeward side of the Andes that block the moist Westerlies.
- A final cause, or range of causes, are human activities. Many of these have given rise to the spread of desert conditions into areas previously fit for agriculture. This is known as **desertification**, and is an increasing problem.

Approximately a third of the world's land surface experiences dry conditions. Semi-arid areas are commonly defined as having a rainfall of less than 500 mm a year, while arid areas have less than 250 mm and extremely arid areas less than 125 mm a year. In addition to low rainfall, dry areas have **variable rainfall**. Variability has important consequences for vegetation cover, farming and the risk of flooding.

(d) Aridity and Land Use

Land use in arid and semi-arid areas is limited. These areas offer limited potential for agriculture, although with irrigation water, such as from rivers like the Nile and the deep aquifers below Libya and south-west USA, farming is possible and profitable. With water there are plants, and the organic content of the soils can develop. In semi-arid areas low-intensity agriculture, such as cattle or sheep ranching, is economically viable without irrigation. For many areas, such as Tunisia, Jordan and Dubai, tourism is seen as having great potential for economic development, on account for the predictable hot, dry conditions. For the same reason, arid and semi-arid climates are also proving to be popular areas for retirement homes (the Sun Belt of the south-west USA).

3 Urban Environments

(a) Urban Influences

Cities transform natural landscapes significantly.

- The expansion of cities reshapes land surfaces and water flows. In the absence of effective land-use management, urbanisation can have serious ecological impacts such as soil erosion, deforestation, and the loss of agricultural land and of sites with valuable ecological functions.

- The 'export' of solid, liquid and airborne pollutants and wastes often brings serious environmental impacts to regions around cities, including damage to fisheries by untreated liquid wastes, land and groundwater pollution from inadequately designed and managed solid waste dumps, and for many of the larger and more industrial cities, acid rain.
- Freshwater resources are being depleted. Many cities have outgrown the capacity of their locality to provide fresh water or have over-used or mismanaged local sources so these are no longer usable. Increasingly distant and costly water sources have to be used, often to the detriment of the regions from which these are drawn.

The greatest concentration of environmental problems occurs in cities experiencing rapid growth (Figure 57). This concentration of problems is referred to as the **Brown Agenda**. It has two main components:

- issues caused by limited availability of land, water and services
- problems such as toxic hazardous waste, pollution of water, air and soil, and industrial 'accidents' such as Bhopal in 1985.

(b) Urban Opportunities and Disadvantages

Urban centres provide many environmental opportunities. High densities and large population concentrations usually lower the costs per household and per enterprise for the provision of infrastructure and services. Cities also have many potential advantages for reducing resource use and waste. For instance, the close proximity of so many water consumers gives greater scope for recycling or directly reusing waste water.

Good environmental management can also limit the tendency for cities to transfer environmental costs to rural areas, for example, through:

- enforcing pollution control to protect water quality in nearby water bodies, safeguarding those who draw water from them, and also fisheries
- an emphasis on 'waste reduction, reuse, recycle' to reduce the volume of wastes that are disposed of in the area around cities
- comprehensive storm and surface drains, and garbage collection systems that reduce sources of water pollution.

The fact that large urban centres have high concentrations of people, enterprises and motor vehicles – and their wastes – can make them very hazardous places in which to live and work. Average life expectancies can be below 40 years, and one child in four may die before the age of 5. The urban poor face the greatest risks as their homes and neighbourhoods generally have the least adequate provision for water supplies, sanitation, drainage, garbage collection and health care.

Many of the most serious diseases in cities are 'environmental' because they are transmitted through disease-causing agents (pathogens) in the

Problems	Causes	Possible solutions
Waste products and waste disposal, e.g. 25% of all urban dwellers in LEDCs have no adequate sanitation and no means of sewage disposal	Solids from paper, packaging and toxic waste increase as numbers and living standards rise Liquid sewage and industrial waste both rise exponentially Contamination and health hazards from poor systems of disposal, e.g. rat infestation and water-borne diseases	Improved public awareness – recycling, etc.; landfill sites, incineration plants Development of effective sewage systems and treatment plants including recycling of brown water for industrial use Rubbish management
Air pollution, e.g. air in Mexico City is 'acceptable' on fewer than 20 days annually!	Traffic, factories, waste incinerators and power plants produce pollutants Some specialist chemical pollution Issues of acid deposition	Closure of old factories and importation of clean technology, e.g. filters Use of cleaner fuels Re-siting of industrial plants, e.g. oil refineries in areas downwind of settlements
Water pollution, e.g. untreated sewage into the Ganga from cities such as Varanasi and into the Thames in the summer of 2004	Leaking sewers, landfill and industrial waste In some LEDCs agricultural pollution from fertilisers and manure is a problem	Control of point sources of pollution at source by regulation and fining; development of mains drainage systems and sewers Removal of contaminated land sites
Water supply, e.g. overuse of groundwater led to subsidence and flooding in Bangkok	Aquifer depletion, ground subsidence and low flow of rivers	Construction of reservoirs, pipeline construction from long-distance catchment, desalination of salt water Water conservation strategies
Transport-related issues, e.g. average speed of traffic in São Paulo is 3 km/hour	Rising vehicle ownership leads to congestion, noise pollution, accidents and ill health due to release of carbon monoxide, nitrogen oxide and, indirectly, low-level ozone Photochemical smog formation closely related to urban sprawl	Introduction of cleaner car technology (unleaded petrol catalytic converters); monitoring and guidelines for various pollution levels; movement from private car to public transport; green transport planning Creation of compact and more sustainable cities

Figure 57 Environmental problems in urban areas

air, water, soil or food, or through insect or animal disease vectors. Many diseases and disease vectors thrive when provision for water, sanitation, drainage, garbage collection and health care is inadequate.

Official statistics often over-state the proportion of urban dwellers adequately served. Many governments assume that all urban dwellers within 100 m of standpipes or latrines are 'adequately served', despite the difficulties of access. They remain classified as 'adequately served' even when water supply is irregular and poor quality. Tens of millions of urban dwellers have no toilet they can use so they either defecate in the open or in plastic bags.

Airborne infections are among the world's leading causes of death. For many, their transmission is aided by overcrowding and inadequate ventilation that is common in the tenements, boarding houses or small shacks in which most low-income urban dwellers live.

The scale and severity of many chemical and physical hazards increase rapidly with urbanisation and industrialisation. While controlling infectious diseases centres on provision of infrastructure and services, reducing chemical and physical hazards is largely achieved by regulating the activities of enterprises and households.

In many urban areas, domestic indoor air pollution from open fires or poorly vented stoves that use coal or biomass fuels has serious health impacts. Lower income households are affected more as people tend to move to cleaner, safer fuels when incomes rise.

There is also a growing need for more effective control of outdoor (ambient) air pollution from industries and motor vehicles. Worldwide, more than 1.5 billion urban dwellers are exposed to levels of ambient air pollution that are above the recommended maximum levels. Urban air pollution problems are particularly pressing in many Indian and Chinese cities.

(c) Water

Urban dwellers in Africa only use 50 litres of water per person per day. In addition, the 'average' price of water is highest in Africa. However, less than 35% of cities in LEDCs have their waste water treated. In countries with economies in transition, 75% of solid wastes are disposed of in open dumps. Nevertheless, there are examples of successful water development schemes.

Efforts by the Chilean government in water and sanitation show that state-run systems can achieve positive results. By 1990, 97% of Chile's urban population had access to safe water, and 80% had access to sanitation. The reasons for the country's success:

- increasing financial investments in the sector
- developing a system for fixing tariffs objectively
- introducing incentives for efficiency.

Between 1988 and 1990, Chilean authorities established a new system for fixing tariffs objectively. The reform permitted the gradual adjustment of tariffs to new, higher levels. The private sector played a role in Chile's water and sanitation sector, but this role was limited and strictly regulated by the central government. There was a big increase in the contracting out of many activities by all companies.

4 Forests and Development

Poor economic policies, population growth and poverty are the main causes of deforestation. Brazil and south-east Asia have seen some of the worst cases of logging. The effects of this are global warming and the eradication of species, many of which will be indigenous to the areas under threat.

To try and control deforestation, there needs to be co-operation and agreement between government, industry, environmentalists and the local population dependent on the forest on creating policies discouraging deforestation.

(a) Developing Rainforests

The world's rainforests are 'owned' by the mainly LEDCs they cover, but at the same time they are a global asset. Cutting them down for profit, or to free land for farming, is a tempting source of income. Left intact, they are sinks that withhold carbon dioxide from the atmosphere, mitigating the problem of human-made global warming, and they are rich storehouses of biodiversity, another global resource. A balance between local and global interests must be struck.

CASE STUDY: DEFORESTATION IN AMAZONIA

The causes and effects of deforestation are widely known, with logging and ranching being the main causes and contributing to a decrease of 15% of the Amazon at a rate of approximately 0.5% per year, and carbon released into the atmosphere being the effect. It is estimated that the carbon released from the deforestation that takes places in Brazil and Indonesia alone, is about 80% of the cuts in carbon emissions required by the Kyoto Protocol from 2008 to 2012.

So, curbing deforestation would have a major impact on the amount of carbon emissions in the atmosphere and, ultimately, on global warming. So how can it be controlled? A number of initiatives have been set up, such as:

- The Amazon Reserves and Protected Areas project. This is a partnership between Brazil's government and international organisations such as the World Bank. The plan is to protect

Figure 58 Highway BR-163, Brazil

14% of the rainforest in areas as yet undisturbed by deforestation through investing $400 million over 10 years.

- The Clean Development Mechanism of the Kyoto Protocol. This offers industries emitting large amounts of carbon the option of donating money to projects that reduce carbon emissions as a way of paying for or offsetting their polluting activities.

However plans such as the BR-163, a 1765-km highway from Santarém, a port on the Amazon River, to Cuiabá, the capital of the state of Mato Grosso, may undermine the efforts to reduce carbon emissions (see Figure 58). While the highway, planned by the Brazilian government, would bring many benefits to trade, for example the delivery cost and time will be significantly reduced for companies using the bumpy roads or congested ports at present, it could also force carbon emissions to rise due to the extensive deforestation needed to make way for the paved road. It is estimated that 30–40% of the Amazon could be deforested due to road building. The paving of the BR-163, will destroy 22,000–49,000 km^2 of forest within 35 years. It is for this reason that this project now involves NGOs, and multinationals, as well as Brazil's government.

However, the Brazilian government does have plans in mind to reduce any possibility of further damage to the forest. They propose to make areas of land off-limits to all but environmentally friendly development, limit development to 40 km either side of the road, reserve land as conservation areas and encourage people to use areas where damage has already been done. These have been called zones of consolidation.

5 Hazards and Development

The case study of flooding in Bangladesh (page 25) illustrates the impacts of hazards on development. Equally a lack of water (drought) hinders development. Similarly, continued volcanic activity in Montserrat threatens the country's economic performance, although there are signs that the island is beginning to turn the corner (see Figure 59).

Montserrat is one of the Leeward Islands chain in the eastern Caribbean. There are least 15 potentially active volcanoes spread along the length of the chain, of which the Soufrière Hills volcano of southern Montserrat is one and the one currently most active. The current eruption of the Soufrière Hills volcano began in 1995.

(a) Economic and Social Development

The capital city Plymouth was abandoned following the 1997 eruption. Temporary government buildings have been built at Brades Estate, in the Carr's Bay/Little Bay area in north-west Montserrat (Figure 60). There has been a huge increase in the provision of housing in St John's, and there have been new schools, crèches and hospitals built. Much of the transport infrastructure has been improved, and there has been investment in the port facilities. FIFA have built a football pitch – this may rate as one of the most attractive pitches in the world! – while the Montserrat government offices have been

* Population 8437
* Population growth rate 8.43% (2002 estimate)
* Birth rate 17.54 per 1000
* Death rate 7.47 per 1000
* Infant mortality rate 7.98 per 1000 live births
* Life expectancy 78.2 years (80.4 years for females, 76.1 years for males)

Figure 59 Key facts on Montserrat

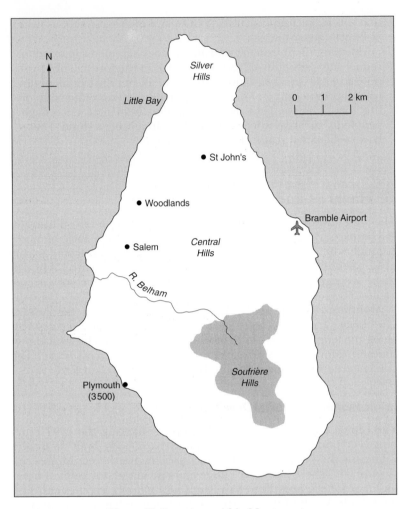

Figure 60 Locations within Montserrat

relocated and rebuilt in St John's. New service industries have developed in Salem, and there has been an increase in ecotourism and adventure tourism.

Prospects for the economy depend largely on public sector construction activity. The UK has launched a 3-year £66 million aid programme (known as the Country Policy Plan, 2001–2003) to help reconstruct the economy. The EU has agreed a £6.5 million grant to help relocate the capital from Plymouth to Little Bay. The southern third of the island is expected to remain uninhabited for at least another decade. Agriculture accounts for 5.4% of the GDP. The lack of suitable land means that it is unlikely that this figure will increase much in future years. By contrast, over 80% of GDP is generated by services and this is likely to increase as the aid programmes continue.

Chapter Summary

- There are many links between the environment and development – poverty, education and health, for example.
- For most people, the impact of climate is the main environmental impact on lifestyle.
- Climate and weather affect many activities.
- Lack of water – aridity – can cause some countries to be under-developed.
- Global climate change will have a major impact on development.
- Policies to combat climate change face many problems.
- Urban environments experience intense environmental problems but they also have greater potential for solving their problems.
- Water is a major problem in many LEDCs.
- Rainforests offer many opportunities for LEDCs (and MEDCs). However, their misuse has global consequences.
- Natural hazards result in some countries remaining undeveloped.

Questions

1. Outline the ways in which climate change may affect development.
2. To what extent do natural hazards limit development?
3. In what ways do urban areas affect their environment?
4. Examine the causes and consequences of deforestation of rainforests.

7 Sustainable Development

KEY TERMS

Sustainable development Sustainable development refers to an improvement in basic living standards without compromising the needs of future generations.
Carrying capacity The maximum impact that an ecosystem can sustain.

1 Sustainability

Sustainable development is development that 'meets the needs of the present without compromising the ability of future generations to meet their own needs' (Brundtland, 1987). It is a process by which human potential (standards of well-being) are improved and the environment (the resource base) is used and managed to supply humanity on a long-term basis. It implies social justice as well as long-term environmental sustainability. The definition suggests that humankind has degraded the planet and must make amends for future generations. The definition is somewhat difficult to comprehend, as it takes in economic issues, ecological concepts, sociological principles and moral rights.

The global economy depends on the natural environment as a source of resources, as a sink for emissions and as a provider of services (e.g. a warm climate offers tourist potential). The capacity of natural systems to provide resources and to absorb increasing levels of pollution is the critical threshold to how far population can increase and the economy expand. One of the most widely used concepts in this regard is the **carrying capacity**. This is the maximum impact that an ecosystem can sustain. In population terms there is a qualitative element too. It is the maximum population that can be sustained without a decline in standards of living.

Acid rain, global warming, desertification and deforestation may reduce our standards of living. In order to be sustainable, the level and rate of resource exploitation should be no greater than the level and rate of natural regeneration of natural systems. However, as population increases so too does demand. As technology increases, the amount of resources exploited increases exponentially. Moreover, with increasing trade and communications there is virtually no region that sustains itself purely with the resources from within its own boundaries. Most regions now depend on the supply of other resources from other regions, and the growth in world trade enables regions to exceed their carrying capacity by importing resources from other regions. A move towards sustainability would require difficult choices, and some fundamental changes in attitudes, values and practices (see Figure 61).

- Respect and care for the community of life
- Improve the quality of human life
- Conserve the Earth's vitality and diversity
- Minimise the depletion of non-renewable resources
- Keep within the Earth's carrying capacity
- Change personal attitudes and practices
- Enable communities to care for their own environments
- Provide a national framework for integrating development and conservation
- Create a global alliance

Figure 61 Principles of sustainable development. *Source*: Park (1997)

2 World Crises

There are a number of interlinked crises that reduce efforts of achieving sustainability. These crises have a social, environmental and political slant. Currently about one-fifth of the world's six billion population live in desperately poor conditions – these are the global 'underclass', those whose lives are at the edge of existence and are continuously close to famine, disease, hunger and death. What is more, the gap between rich and poor is increasing. It is not just a question of GDP per head. Economic indicators fail to take into account the pollution and the depletion of natural resources. As developing countries provide many of the raw materials for economic development in the west, the developing world is disadvantaged even more.

The environmental crises are a result of the limited amount of resources that the Earth contains and the rate at which they are being destroyed. There is a social aspect to the destruction of resources: the 20% of the world's population that live in developed countries consume 80% of the world's resources, whereas the 80% of the population that live in developing countries use only 20% of the resources. The world's environmental crises are increasingly rapid, and cross international boundaries. For example, the transfer of radioactive waste and acid rain across western Europe, and the build up of greenhouse gasses in the atmosphere are all issues that do not recognise borders, whether terrestrial or national.

Political conflict in the form of war, ethnic cleansing, refugee crises, trading blocs, trade wars and economic sanctions have increased. These seriously hamper the prospects of achieving sustainable development.

The United Nations Conference on the Human Environment (Stockholm, 1972) was a turning point for a better understanding of human impact on the environment, and implicitly, sustainability. At the same time the influential *Limits to Growth* model was produced, this drew attention to shortages of natural resources, increases in pollution, and the eventual collapse of human society some time around 2100.

More recently environmental issues have come to the fore in the World Commission on Environment and Development through its

- **Sustainable development:** development that meets the needs of the present without compromising the ability of future generations to meet their own needs
- **Precautionary principle:** this broadly demands that if an activity or substance carries a significant risk of environmental damage it should either not proceed or be used, or should be adopted at only the minimum essential level, and with maximum practical safeguards
- **Polluter pays principle (PPP):** that polluters should pay the full costs of pollution-reduction measures decided upon by public authorities to ensure that the environment is in an acceptable state. More recently the PPP has been extended to accidental pollution
- **Shared responsibility:** the principle involves not so much a choice of action at one administrative level to the exclusion of others, but rather a mixing of actors and instruments at different administrative levels, enterprises or indeed the general public or consumers
- **Environmental impact assessment (EIA):** the necessary preliminary practice of evaluating the risks posed by a certain project before granting permission for a development
- **Best available technology (BAT):** signifies the latest or state-of-the-art techniques and technologies in the development of activities, processes and their methods of operation, which minimise emissions to the environment
- **Environmental quality standard (EQS):** the set of requirements that must be fulfilled at a given time by a given environment or particular part thereof
- **Integrated pollution prevention and control (IPC):** to provide for measures and procedures to prevent (wherever practicable) or to minimise emissions from industrial installations so as to achieve a high level of protection for the environment as a whole. The IPC concept arose when it became clear that approaches to controlling emissions in one medium alone may encourage shifting the burden of pollution across other environmental media. This concept requires that emission limit values are set within the aim of not breaching EQS: only when EQSs or other relevant guidelines are missing can emission levels be based on BAT

Figure 62 Concepts for environmental protection. *Source*: EEA (1995)

publication *Our Common Future* (also known as the Brundtland Report) and at the Rio conference (United Nations Conference on Environment and Development, 1982). Environmental problems are increasingly seen as being international. Ozone depletion, acid rain, global warming and desertification have an effect on scores of countries, even those that are not causing any of the damage. One of the major outcomes of the Rio conference was the action plan for the 1990s and the beginning of the twenty-first century. This is commonly referred to as Agenda 21. Agenda 21 refers to detailed plans and strategies in all countries, from local governments up to national governments, aimed at achieving sustainable development. Strategies vary and include regulation (through legal and economic controls), management, co-operation, monitoring and assessment. A fundamental aim of the Rio conference was to replace environmentally damaging practices with sustainable and environmentally friendly forms of development (see Figure 62).

The key issues that are now taken more seriously are:

- inter-generational implications of patterns of resource use: how effectively do decisions about the use of natural resources preserve an environmental heritage or estate for the benefit of future generations?
- equity concerns: who has access to resources? How fairly are available resources allocated between competing claimants?
- time horizons: how much are resource allocation decisions orientated towards short-term economic gain or long-term environmental stability?

Figure 63 Issues within sustainable development. *Source*: Park (1997)

3 Role of Local Agenda 21

As a result of the Earth Summit national governments are obliged to formulate national plans or strategies for sustainable development – Agenda 21. It is *people* who do development, not governments, and therefore sustainable development is a local activity. Moreover, all people, however poor, have some ability, however constrained, of changing what they do, in small ways. Managing and preserving the environment has a number of advantages.

Local authorities are beginning to translate the global sustainability agenda – Agenda 21 – into local action. Just as global sustainability cannot exist without national sustainable policies, national Agenda 21 is incomplete without local Agenda 21 (see Figure 63).

4 Sustainable Development in South Africa

(a) Clean Water: A Basic Human Right

The constitution of South Africa allows every person has right to clean water. The Department of Water Affairs and Forestry's Community Water Supply and Sanitation Programme (CWSS), established in 1994, has provided about 6.5 million people a basic water supply. By 2002, 27 million people had access to clean water and a policy giving poor families 6000 litres of free water every month was implemented in late 2000.

(b) Sanitation

One in two South Africans has no access to adequate sanitation facilities – either no facilities, or an unsafe pit or bucket toilet – and so there is a clear need to address the sanitation problems. Acute diarrhoea is a direct consequence of poor water and sanitation provision. Diarrhoea kills more than 50,000 South African children every year and affects millions more.

- Education: adult literacy is up from 87% to 92%. 23% of South Africans have passed the matric examination, compared to 14% in 1994
- Health: South Africa's malaria control programme was recognised by the World Health Organization as the best in the southern African region in 2001–2002
- Water: 83.4% of South African households have access to clean water. Since the beginning of 1999, four million more South Africans have got access to clean running water, with a 62% improvement in rural households with running water available either in the house or on the plot
- Alien vegetation: South Africa's Working for Water project is the biggest conservation endeavour on the continent, tackling the scourge of alien vegetation head-on while employing in the region of 18,000 people
- The Transfrontier park that spans South Africa, Mozambique and Zimbabwe is the world's first conservation initiative of its kind. The 38,600 km^2 park will be bigger than the Yellowstone National Park in the USA, and even bigger than Switzerland, Belgium or Taiwan.
- Urban forest: the trees of Johannesburg form one of the largest urban forests in the world

Figure 64 Sustainable South Africa factfile

In early 2002 the Water, Sanitation and Hygiene campaign (WASH), a global health programme, was initiated to highlight the importance of washing hands after toilet use in reducing disease. In 2001 the department spent £10 million constructing 50,000 pit latrines and will continue to do so until all people have access to basic sanitation within 15 years.

Mvula Trust, the country's largest water and sanitation NGO, is managing and implementing sanitation programmes in six provinces; has helped over 10,000 households to improve their sanitation facilities; has worked in over 500 villages; has implemented sanitation projects in over 100 schools; and has distributed over £3 million to support sanitation services in South Africa.

Although a water-borne sewage system – where flushable toilets pipe water through underground pipes to sewage depots long distances away – may seem preferable, high maintenance and running costs render this option inappropriate for many communities. Increasingly, Mvula Trust and the Department of Water Affairs and Forestry are looking at dry sanitation options – either pit latrines or urine diversion toilets. Pit latrines or 'long drops' are often the most appropriate solution: if well managed, they are not harmful to the environment or users.

Ventilated improved pit toilets, as they are now called, allow the urine to drain off, enabling the faeces to dry up and decompose safely. Problems arise, however, if the latrines are sunk into the ground water, causing contamination.

Few have heard of 'urine diversion' toilets, but these are likely to become a regular phenomenon in many homes in the years to come. Mvula Trust has so far introduced 2500 in the country, and the project is gaining momentum. The toilet separates faeces and urine. The urine is diverted into a special pot in the toilet and siphoned underground through a thin pipe, where it soaks into the ground, fertilising the soil.

The waste collects in a 25-litre bucket under the toilet and is treated each time with a mix of ash and soil, which helps to dehydrate it. Once a month the bucket is emptied and either burnt or collected into a compost bin, where it is treated with more soil, ash and other waste, such as kitchen organics (fruit and vegetable peels). It can then be used as compost in the garden or vegetable patch.

(c) Food and Trees

Food and Trees for Africa (FTFA) is a fast-growing NGO that promotes greening and food security through Permaculture. FTFA has three key programmes: Trees for Homes, Eduplant and the Urban Greening Foundation. Trees for Homes espouses the view that 'a house is not a home without a tree'. FTFA aims to improve the quality of life of the poor by providing plant material, environmental awareness and education for those living in low-cost housing developments.

(d) Trees for Homes

The majority of South Africa's disadvantaged people continue to live in these poorly designed and impoverished urban and peri-urban housing settlements. Growing trees and other plants in the townships brightens the environment, prevents soil erosion and provides wind breaks, as well as food, income and activities for many unemployed people.

(e) Eduplant

Eduplant is a nationwide project that teaches schools about permaculture – a system of farming and gardening that combines animals, plants, buildings, local people and the landscape in a way that recycles nutrients and waste, replicates nature as much as possible and generates more energy than it uses. Although food production is one of its central themes, it is also about energy-efficient buildings, waste-water treatment, recycling and land conservation. Its design principles mimic nature, giving high yields for low-energy inputs, and apply equally to urban and rural dwellers. Now hundreds of schools have started their own income-generating organic food gardens. Often the entire community gets involved, with unemployed parents helping out. Schools have come up with innovative plans to grow food, recycle waste and improve their school environments.

(f) Goats and Rural Development

Podi-Boswa (Pty) Ltd has given much-needed hope to a north-west province community traumatised by the closure of local platinum mines. Podi-Boswa – which means 'goat, our inheritance' – provides £150 per goat from the animal's meat, milk and skin. With the support of the World Conservation Union (IUCN), the Agricultural Research Council and the Department of Trade and Industry's Community Public–Private Partnership Programme, Podi-Boswa combines the power of indigenous knowledge and the value of a natural resource to give a sustainable livelihood to over 1000 people who had been living on the brink of despair.

The project is a successful rural development project that could provide a good model for sustainable development in similar outlying areas in South Africa. The business model could also be used in other developing countries where subsistence agriculture and farming is common. Podi-Boswa started in 2000, and has grown to the point where, currently, it involves almost 30 villages in the province, and trains young people to make goat leather handbags, belts and purses. These products are marketed to the South African tourism industry.

(g) Working for Water

Working for Water employs 18,000 people (who would otherwise be jobless) to chop down and clear invading alien species, including wattle, gums, pines, hakea and triffid weed. Many of these invasive species consume vast quantities of water, thus depleting precious supplies. They also fuel devastating fires that can destroy indigenous species and cause costly damage. According to the US government, invasive alien species have effectively wiped out 4% of global GDP. This is two-and-a-half times Africa's combined GDP. After habitat destruction by humans, invasives are the second biggest potential cause of species extinction in the world.

Working for Water, which has an annual budget of £40 million, co-operates with a range of government departments. Invading alien plants destroy the productive potential of land, contributing to poverty, unemployment and social problems. Alien species altogether are estimated to consume 3300 million cubic metres of water, which amounts to 7% of South Africa's annual run-off.

The fight against these tough aliens appears to be a battle of epic proportions. For example, a lightly infested hectare of land could cost about £10 to clear, whereas the same land left for the next 15 years, would cost 40 times as much to clear.

5 Sustainable Tourism Development in Barbados

Tourism is the main industry in Barbados accounting for approximately 50% of GDP. It is important therefore that the environment is protected as much as possible. The National Commission on Sustainable Development (in Barbados) recognises that tourism is the economic engine of Barbados, employing thousands of people. However,

Barbados' tourism industry has not always evolved along sustainable paths. Concerns for environmental conservation and protection are crucial, since the natural environment dominates the Barbados tourism product. The Commission recommends that an assessment of the carrying capacity be determined using different scenarios:

- business as usual
- more conservative use of natural resources
- voluntary environmental management
- regulated environmental management
- economic incentives and instruments to promote environmental compliance.

Marketing programmes promoting Barbados as a tourism destination stress the country's efforts to promote sustainable tourism. Visitors to the island are encouraged to comply with voluntary or regulated environmental management efforts. All those in the tourism sector are required to implement environmental management programmes for their individual operation.

CASE STUDY: SUSTAINABLE TOURISM AT CASUARINA BEACH CLUB, BARBADOS

The Casuarina Beach Club is one of the best examples of how sustainable tourism can operate. The hotel has shown considerable environmental awareness and responsibility. For example:

- sound environmental practices, meeting the internationally recognised Green Globe 21 criteria
- the forging of partnerships with the national and local governments, NGOs and the local community
- conservation of natural resources
- environmental awareness training for the staff, fellow hoteliers, learning institutes and schools
- massive reductions in waste by composting and other reuse and recycling initiatives (Figure 65)
- limited chemical use in preferences for natural alternatives
- promotion of local culture, history, music and furniture
- protection of turtle nesting habitats
- revegetation projects
- conservation of coastal forest strip to act as a hurricane defence.

The guidelines that Casuarina follow for environmental improvement are based on Agenda 21 – the comprehensive programme of action adopted by 182 governments at the Rio Earth Summit in 1992. Casuarina also belongs to CAST (Caribbean Alliance for Sustainable Tourism).

In March 2000 Casuarina achieved Green Globe 21 certification – an award given by the England-based environmental management programme for travel and tourism.

(a) Waste Minimisation

Casuarina has adopted the policy of 'reduce, reuse and recycle'. Separation of garbage is apparent throughout the property. The hotel has reduced the amount of packaging by contacting suppliers and requesting less packaging. Individual portions of ketchup and butter, for example, are not provided in the restaurants. Instead hard, reusable bottles and containers are used. Paper towels have been replaced by hand driers. Large shampoo and conditioner dispensers have replaced individual sachets.

The biggest reuse initiative has been the collection of 320 plastic containers in which the cooking oil was delivered, and after modification, these now facilitate the garbage collection in the guest rooms. Composting of food is facilitated by means of four compostumblers. Recycling initiatives include the manufacture of *pot pourri* from cut flowers, and recycled paper from waste generated on the property.

Meet Muriel at the Flower Cart

Muriel is a disabled person aiming to achieve financial independence by running her own flower business. Please help her by purchasing some flowers for your room. If you do not wish to take home the flower vase you may return it for resale.
This is joint venture of the National Disabilities Unit of Barbados and the Casuarina Beach Club

Figures 65 Examples (above and opposite) of sustainable development at the Casuarina Beach Club, Barbados

Water loss is reduced by installing low-flow devices on the showers and taps. Beach and poolside showers are fitted with 'pull-chain flush valve' systems. Waste water from the beach showers is used to irrigate the gardens. The well water on the property is used to irrigate the grounds. There are signs in the hotels rooms regarding the choice of frequency of changing the towels, which reduces the consumption of water.

Other initiatives include:

- the hotel purchases from local producers as much as possible
- only degradable plastic bags are used in the hotel
- local handicapped people are employed in the hotel.

Chapter Summary

- Sustainable development refers to an improvement in basic living standards without compromising the needs of future generations.
- In South Africa many people lack clean water and/or proper sanitation.
- There are a number of programmes aimed at developing clean water resources to South Africans – some of these are government initiatives, others NGOs.
- In parts of South Africa's urban areas trees are being planted to improve the environment and to provide a source of food.
- Podi-Boswa is a good example of a successful rural development scheme.
- In Barbados, the environment is the key to the tourist industry.
- Maintaining a healthy environment is vital to attracting tourists.
- The Barbados government is committed to sustainable development.
- At a local level, the Casuarina Beach Club illustrates many of the ways in which sustainable development can be achieved.

Questions

1. In what ways can development be unsustainable?
2. With the use of examples show how sustainable development can be achieved.
3. To what extent is it possible for tourism to be sustainable?

Bibliography

Binns, J.A. and Lynch, K. (1998) 'Sustainable food production in sub-Saharan Africa: the significance of urban and per-urban agriculture', *Journal for International Development* **10**(6): 777–93.

Brundtland, W. (1987) *Our Common Future*, Oxford: Oxford University Press.

Desai, V. (1995) *Community Participation and Slum Housing: A Study of Bombay*, London: Sage.

Dicken, P. (1992) *Global Shift*, London: Paul Chapman.

EEA (1995) *Europe's Environment*, Copenhagen: European Environment Agency (EEA).

Ellis, F. (2000) *Rural Livelihoods and Diversity in Developing Countries*, Oxford: Oxford University Press.

Food and Agricultural Organization (FAO) (1996) *World Food Summit: Rome Declaration on World Food Security and World Food Summit Plan of Action*, Rome: FAO.

Food and Agricultural Organization (FAO) (1999) *The State of Food Insecurity in the World*, Rome: FAO ('Who, why and where' of hungry people and food security, and recent statistics).

Frank, A.G. (1966) *Capitalism and Underdevelopment in Latin America*, New York: Monthly Review Press.

Friedmann, J. (1986) 'The world city hypothesis', *Development and Change* **17**: 69–83.

Gilbert, A.G. and Gugler, J. (1992) *Cities, Poverty and Development: Urbanization in the Third World*, 2nd edn, Oxford: Oxford University Press.

Goudie, A. editor (1994) *The Encyclopaedic Dictionary of Physical Geography*, Oxford: Blackwell.

Goulet, O. (1971) *The Cruel Choice: A New Theory on the Concept of Development*, New York, Atheneum.

Gugler, J. editor (1997) *Cities in the Developing World: Issues, Theory and Policy*, Oxford: Oxford University Press.

Hardoy, J.E., Mitlin, D. and Satterthwaite, D. (2001) *Environmental Problems in an Urbanizing World*, London: Earthscan.

Knox, P. and Taylor, P. editors (1995) *World Cities in a World System*, Cambridge: Cambridge University Press.

Legrain, P. (2002) *Open World: The Truth About Globalisation*, London: Abacus.

Lipton, M. (1977) *Why Poor People Stay Poor: Urban Bias in World Development*, London: Temple Smith.

Mullen, J. (1999) *Rural Poverty, Empowerment and Sustainable Livelihoods*, Aldershot: Ashgate.

Nagle, G. (1998) *Development and Underdevelopment*, Cheltenham: Nelson.

Nagle, G. and Spencer, K. (1996) *A Geography of the European Union*, Oxford: Oxford University Press.

Nagle, G. (2003) *AS and A Level Geography for Edexcel Specification B*, Oxford: Oxford University Press.

Nederveen Pieterse, I. (2000) 'After post development', *Third World Quarterly* **21**(2): 175–91.

Park, C. (1997) *The Environment: Principles and Applications*, London: Routledge.

Perroux, F. (1971) Note on the concept of growth poles. In Livingstone, T. *Economic Policy for Development: Selected Reading*, London: Penguin.

Portés, A., Dore-Cabral, C. and Landoff, P. editors (1997) *The Urban Caribbean: Transition to a New Global Economy*, Baltimore, MD: Johns Hopkins University Press.

Potter, R. and Lloyd-Evans, S. (1998) *The City in the Developing World*, London: Longman.

Potter, R.B. (1995) *Housing and the State in the Eastern Caribbean*, Kingston, Jamaica: University of the West Indies Press.

Sen, A. (1981) *Poverty and Famines*, Oxford: Oxford University Press.

Sen, A (1983) 'Development: which way now?', *Economic Journal* **93**: 745–62.

Simon, D. (1993) *Cities, Capital and Development: African Cities in the World Economy*, London: Belhaven.

United Nations Conference on Trade and Development (UNCTAD) (1999) *World Investment Report: Foreign Direct Investment and the Challenge of Development*, New York: United Nations.

United Nations Development Programme (UNDP) (1998) *Globalization and Liberalization*, New York: United Nations Development Programme.

United Nations Population Fund (2004) *The State of World Population 2004*, New York; United Nations (also at http://www.unfpa.org/swp/swpmain.htm).

Wallerstein, I. (1974) *The Modern World System*, New York: Academic Press.

Waters, M. (2001) *Globalisation*, London: Routledge.

World Resources Institute (2004) *World Resources 2000–04: Decisions for the Earth*, United Nations Environment Programme, World Resources Institute and the World Bank (also at http://www.governance.wri.org/pubs_description.cfm?PublD = 3764).

Useful Websites

2004 crisis in Sudan

From the UN: www.un.org/depts/ocha/cap/sudan.html
From the Sudanese government: www.sudan.gov.sd/english.htm

AIDS crisis

For disaggregated data on AIDS from the Human Development Reports: http://sedac.ciesin.columbia.edu/hdr/

National human development reports

For national human development reports online see http://hdr.undp.org

Index